# Horizon

*MARCH, 1959* • *VOLUME I, NUMBER 4*

# HORIZON
## A Magazine of the Arts

*MARCH, 1959* • *VOLUME I, NUMBER 4*

PUBLISHER
James Parton

EDITOR
Joseph J. Thorndike, Jr.

MANAGING EDITOR
William Harlan Hale

ASSOCIATE EDITOR
Ralph Backlund

ASSISTANT EDITORS
Margery Darrell
Hilde Heun
Ada Pesin
Jane Wilson

EDITORIAL ASSISTANTS
Robert C. Agee, Caroline Backlund,
Gertrudis Feliu, Mary Ann Pfeiffer,
Judith Shaw, Nancy Teass, Martha Thomson

ART DIRECTOR
Irwin Glusker
*Assistant:* Richard B. Browner

ADVISORY BOARD
Gilbert Highet, *Chairman*
Frederick Burkhardt          Oliver Jensen
Marshall B. Davidson       Jotham Johnson
Alfred Frankfurter       Richard M. Ketchum
J. H. Plumb

CIRCULATION DIRECTOR
Richard V. Benson

HORIZON is published every two months by
American Horizon, Inc., a subsidiary of American
Heritage Publishing Co., Inc., 551 Fifth Avenue,
New York 17, N. Y.
    Single Copies: $3.95
Annual Subscriptions: $18.00 in the U.S. & Can.
                $19.00 elsewhere

Second-Class postage paid at New York, N. Y.

HORIZON welcomes contributions but can assume
no responsibility for such unsolicited material.

COVER: The water color *Personnages devant le Soleil* by Joan Miró, the Catalan painter,
shows a red sun in an infinite sky of white in front of which stand two enigmatic figures.
The exuberant Miró often uses elements of nature, the sun, moon, and birds in his "cosmic
children's corner" described in an article by Pierre Schneider on page 70. The painting,
done in 1942, is in a private collection in Basel, Switzerland.

FRONTISPIECE: *The Joys and Woes of the Crinoline* are illustrated in this marvelously
satirical German print of the 1850's. A theory to explain such extremes in fashion cycles
is presented by Dwight E. Robinson in his article beginning on page 62.

*By* HERBERT J. MULLER

*A symbol of our incomplete knowledge of the past, the giant statue of Emperor Constantine the Great in Rome survives only in fragments.*

# MISUSES OF THE PAST

### HISTORY DISOBEYS THE LAWS THAT

### MANY A HISTORIAN WRITES FOR IT

Writing in the middle of the last century, the historian Froude declared that "the one great Bible which cannot lie is the history of the human race." Americans have lately made this Bible a best seller too. "History is bunk," Henry Ford had said in the 1920's, the boom days when men believed that they had escaped from history, by progress, and that the past was something dead and done with. Today the past has become so popular that it got even me into the paperbacks—made me a kind of poor man's Toynbee. So I should add at once that this sudden interest in history is not really flattering to historians. The plainest reason for it is that men are no longer so proud of the history we have been making, no longer confident that it has been a progress, no longer sure where we are going or why. They are looking for the answers, which once upon a time they thought they knew. They are reading the great Bible anxiously, not reverently.

The trouble remains that this Bible can lie, or at least can yield meanings as radically different and often as dubious as those that Christians have found in their Scriptures. For the inalterable past—all that men have done that can never be undone and has made us what we are—is still not simply behind us, objectively *there* for all to see or read. It is within us. It is an image that changes with our image of ourselves, that differs as we differ. We are creatures of the past, and may suffer from its tyranny; but we are also its creators, and may suffer more from the tyranny of a mythical past. The history that most men know is in fact largely bunk. My present concern is with grossly simplified versions of the past that make the modern world more unintelligible, or more intolerable.

Eminent historians themselves have authorized such simplicities for understandable reasons. Henry Adams remarked

5

that any historian who was not a pedestrian fact-finder naturally dreamed of discovering some grand law governing man's history comparable to Newton's law of gravitation; and by now we have a considerable choice in grand designs or dreams. In the last century Lord Acton, a deeply religious liberal, could still see in Liberty (which he habitually capitalized) the main theme of man's entire history, the key to "every nation, every epoch, every religion, every history." The growth of liberty was the measure of human progress—an idea the more inspiring to him because Progress (also capitalized by Acton) was as he saw it underwritten by Providence. Today Acton's faith is likely to seem naïve, even though he himself fully respected the power of conservative opposition. Other seekers of grand designs have generally had much less trouble finding or imposing their formulas—even when these have seemed uncongenial. In our own time, Oswald Spengler and Arnold Toynbee in particular have forced all history into neat patterns with a remorseless consistency that outrages most other historians but awes many readers.

Today the most obvious example of historical mythmaking is the nationalistic dogma that in all countries makes men arrogant and self-righteous. Americans can readily recall its dangers in prewar Germany, which had been taught by Treitschke and other historians to believe in its superior, manifest national destiny. But we Americans are less aware of possible conceit in our own national habit of proclaiming that we are the greatest nation on earth—a piece of news that the rest of the world may wish we would keep to ourselves now and then. Acton's faith was far removed from a popular image of American greatness, a fable of rugged individualists on the frontier, uncontaminated by foreign influences, giving birth to a 100-per-cent American spirit and going on to conquer a continent and to make the most spectacular progress of all time—progress still more wondrous because it was of an automatic kind that somehow emerged all by itself as everybody went about his private business, made money, and had fun. What made it automatic was economic freedom, the cornerstone of the American Way; and trouble began only when New Dealers started taking to un-American ideas. Herbert Hoover sounded the moral of the fable: "Our American system cannot be made to work part free and part regimented." In Washington such noises still pass for thought; so it seems necessary to observe that in America, as in all other democracies, business has been subject to increasing regulation over the last hundred years, during which time industrial progress has been most marked, and that when it was most thoroughly regimented, in World War II, it worked most spectacularly, doubling the national output within a few years.

Yet this was no simple success story either. It has raised more difficult issues that give thoughtful men deeper misgivings. Regimentation is indeed the order of the day—in business, labor, and entertainment as well as in government.

It has resulted naturally from an industrial revolution that nobody planned but that called out increasing organization and standardization throughout the whole society. It has not only antiquated the gospel of rugged individualism but has produced growing pressures against any real individuality, breeding such types as the "organization man" and the "other-directed" man. It leads many to fear that if we manage to escape catastrophe, we are inexorably bound for something like the brave new world of Aldous Huxley. Such fears point to the growing popularity of views that deny us any real control of our history and any reasonable choice in futures. Such views may make the simple faith of Herbert Hoover seem healthy by contrast. It is with these that I am chiefly concerned here.

In general, they reflect our fuller awareness of the deep, impersonal, unconscious processes in history, as in an industrial revolution that nobody planned. Up to a point such views may be quite sound. The danger point is marked by their common appeal to the "laws" of history—a signal for high, wide, and unhandsome generalization.

In the Communist world these are still iron laws that guarantee progress to a classless society and meanwhile justify violence and tyranny—iron methods of disposing of people who get in the way of this progress. In the democratic world, where few except visionary Marxists can any longer believe in an inevitable progress, the laws may be like those of Spengler, which instead make inevitable the death of our civilization, consistent with a supposedly invariable cycle of growth and decay in all civilizations. Meanwhile they proclaim a "coming Caesarism," or despotism. Or they may be religious laws like Toynbee's, which allow for a kind of spiraling progress as dying civilizations give birth to higher religions, bringing men closer to the One True God. But these also unfortunately require the periodic death of whole civilizations and indicate that we are most likely doomed, our sole hope lying in religion.

Typically they are more or less deterministic laws that drastically limit our choice in possible futures, if they give us any choice at all, and discourage rational effort to make history to suit ourselves. They reinforce the tendencies in fashionable literary and intellectual circles to despair of our godless civilization, condemn all its works, and scorn the idea of progress, especially in the name of Original Sin. Some men are taking an odd pleasure in insisting that man is first and last an incorrigible creature of original sin.

Now, we are indeed creatures of an inalterable past and cannot make any kind of history we have a mind to. Our choice is limited by irreversible tendencies. We might prefer to return to a simple agricultural society, for instance, or the survivors (if any) of a new world war might be forced to do so; but meanwhile there is no going back. It is inconceivable that men will deliberately call a halt to science and give up their machines, upon which now depend the lives of hundreds of millions. We are forced to work within the

# Lord Acton saw liberty
## as the key to history

*Liberty was one of the great, inflaming ideas of the nineteenth century. It overturned governments, inspired poets, and gave themes to artists—even those who were not actively interested in politics, like the French painter Delacroix. He painted his* Liberty Leading the People, *above, to glorify the spirit of the French Revolution of 1830. Today we are inclined to be uneasy in the presence of personified abstractions, but to the great English scholar Lord Acton (1834-1902) this would have seemed an entirely natural expression of the guiding principle of history.*

*Acton is a currently stylish hero among those who require history to show an over-all meaning. In England, at least, his latter-day admirers are numerous enough to form a cult, and they are now proclaiming him one of the greatest historians of the past century.*

*Great he undoubtedly was—but he taught more history than he wrote. The few volumes that bear his name are merely collections of lectures and articles put together after his death. And his long-contemplated* History of Liberty, *for which he assembled some 25,000 notes, has been called the greatest book that was never written.*

*Less doctrinaire than Marx, Spengler, or Toynbee, he did not try to impose a system on history. But he did think that civilization had moved along a definite course in a single direction—upward. This was Progress. And the propulsive force had been Liberty. In his view it was the most profound of the causes that had transformed society; and because he was essentially optimistic and not afraid of moral judgments, he believed that—with a few setbacks—each succeeding transformation had been better than the one before.*

conditions of industrialism, in a world that will continue to be revolutionary for as long as we can foresee. Yet I believe that within such limits the future is still open, its course up to us, and that history gives no reason to believe that we are inevitably doomed or damned. I suspect that many who are attacking the idea of progress, especially on religious grounds, are not fully aware of the implications of their attitude. For if man is as naturally depraved as some say, he is simply not fit for freedom and there can be no hope for a free society. And if we lose our hope of progress, we are pretty sure to lose our freedoms too—or more precisely, we will already have lost them.

I now propose, at any rate, to begin at the beginning, to give some consideration to history as a branch of knowledge and to the reasons why the great Bible is silent on the destiny of man.

Although few historians today would say what many did in the last century, namely that history is or ought to be a pure science, this idea is still in the air we breathe. Scholars often try to confine themselves to fact-finding, declaring that it is not their business to judge, and shy away in virginal fright from concepts of "value" as scientifically unchaste. As the ordinary man sees it, history gives us the facts and the facts speak for themselves; let's stick to the facts, he says. Actually, of course, the facts never speak for themselves. The historian always has to explain or interpret them. He cannot record the great Bible from nobody's point of view, any more than he can take a God's-eye view of it. And he cannot help judging, beginning with his selection of the pertinent and the most important facts.

Just how he decides this is not too clear. Historians used to concentrate on political and military events, or "drum and trumpet" history, paying little attention to the economic facts that have lately come to seem important. Thus everybody has heard of the Crusades, but few have heard of a possibly more important event of the same period and certainly a more beneficial one for mankind—the invention of spectacles in the thirteenth century by an obscure Italian, who thereby enabled many men to make better use of their eyes and heads. Saint Francis and Dante also seem important to us, though they had no apparent influence to speak of on either political or economic developments. So do Michelangelo, Shakespeare, Spinoza, Bach, and many others who made little if any difference in the main march of events. Importance, then, seems to have something to do with cultural values. In any case, for the sake of the very objectivity and impartiality that historians properly aspire to, we should remember that their works not only are to some extent personal interpretations, colored by their philosophical predispositions, but are more profoundly influenced by the climate of opinion in their age.

Here we might profit by heeding the old-fashioned Lord Acton, a Victorian who insisted on the necessity of strict moral judgment and deplored the common tendency of historians "to debase the moral currency" by explaining and condoning the crimes of the past as matters of local custom, products of "the times." If his own judgments may have been too simple and severe (as he himself confessed in his last days), they were always aboveboard and likely to be fair because he was not at all self-righteous, unlike some statesmen who mistake the rehearsal of earnest platitudes for an effort of thought. He was at least not deceiving himself as "scientific" historians are wont to do (the supposedly objective German historians of Acton's time were mostly serving the cause of nationalism). The many honest historians who try not to judge, and whose pages are strewn with judgments, might be more honest if they said in so many words that, like Lord Acton, they believe hypocrisy, fraud, treachery, torture, and murder are evil things. It is possible to excuse faults and errors without condoning the common crimes of history.

At any rate, the impossibility of a pure, unvarnished history becomes plainer when we look into the familiar idea of "cause." The historian always looks for causes and consequences, or connections between the facts; how does he make out these connections? They are not visible links or threads; they cannot be isolated, examined, measured, or tested. Presumably he makes them out by using something like intuition, insight, or common sense—which may be the limited sense of a particular age. And though his explanations may be plausible enough, the trouble remains that there is a whole web of possible connections, a complex of material and spiritual factors, so that different historians assign different causes—up to fifty, for example, for the fall of Rome. The trouble gets worse because many historians tend to speak of the "real" or the "ultimate" cause, as if some connections were stamped with a quality of superior realness. Thus we may now read that the real cause of the Civil War was not the issue of slavery but an economic conflict between North and South. The fact remains that a historian cannot operate on causes by any strictly scientific method, cannot verify his explanations, and above all cannot lay any claim to knowledge of an ultimate cause or *the* explanation.

We need not wonder when a study of the annual addresses of presidents of the American Historical Association, from 1884 to 1945, revealed that the various presidents disagreed about all their basic concepts. They agreed only on the idea that the subject of history is broad and rich. We need not scoff either—I, for one, also wish to keep history broad and rich. I would object to the now-popular "laws" of history if only because they invariably narrow and impoverish it. But here again the plain truth is that historians have been unable to agree on any comprehensive laws, and for a plain reason: they have no means whatever of verifying them.

None of these popular laws are scientific laws comparable

The Mexican muralist Diego Rivera painted this swarming pictorial roster of the villains and heroes of recent history, as defined by the disciples of Karl Marx. Among his villains: Wilson, Rockefeller, Clemenceau, the Czar.

His heroes: Lenin, Trotsky, Eugene V. Debs. Like Lord Acton—but how differently!— Marx saw history as a progression, with each stage in its forward march unfolding inexorably from the last. For him the motive

power was the struggle to control the means of production—a collision between classes that, in the Marxian view, was bound to engulf the world. And Marx had no doubt of the outcome: the victory of the proletariat.

to those in physics; they are not statements of invariable relations applying uniformly to all past events or making possible certain predictions of future events. All are man-made laws that man may break, as he cannot break the law of gravitation. Some, like Spengler's and Toynbee's, come down to pure conjecture, supported by a ruthlessly systematic disregard of inconvenient facts, which in the natural sciences would convict a man of dishonesty. Others may state statistical probabilities, as about pendulum swings or business cycles. Still others amount to rough generalizations, like proverbs. Thus Lord Acton's famous observation: "Power tends to corrupt, and absolute power corrupts absolutely."

This observation—so obviously true, but still only partially true—may do for a test. To begin with, it points to a fatal limitation of Marx's theory, namely his neglect of the eternal problem of political power. He, and Lenin after him, assumed that there would be no such problem once the revolution had been won—proletarian dictators were immune to corruption—so their theory made no provision for the brutal despotism of Stalin. This in turn points to the all too familiar but variable and incalculable "human" factors that invalidate any purely economic interpretation of history—the genius or the failings of rulers and generals; the devotion or the sluggishness of followers; the uses of knowledge and intelligence; the power of ideals; the power of sentiment, passion, or prejudice, racial, national, religious. Such factors should also warn us against the inveterate tendency to seek a single principle of explanation, in keeping with the philosophical tradition that the One is a more illustrious kind of reality than the Many.

We may now link Marx with the many respectable conservatives who also make economics the primary consideration, arguing that business comes first, sanctifying the law of supply and demand, and celebrating economic freedom as the most fundamental freedom. Marx and the conservatives both throw light on our own society, which has emphasized economic interests and the profit motive far more than almost all societies of the past. For the same reason both are poor guides to an understanding either of history or of human nature.

Yet Lord Acton's truism remains a half-truth and can be misleading. Power is as necessary as it is dangerous, necessary even for the maintenance of the liberty to which Lord Acton was so ardently devoted. There is no virtue in feeble or impotent government. While the fear of power has led to democracy—a political system designed to keep rulers responsible—it has also supported the fallacy that every gain in power by the government is necessarily at the expense of individual freedom. The power of government can be used to give people more effective freedom, for example through public education and unemployment relief. And if power tends to corrupt, it may also make a man more sober and responsible, as it did with many of the greater rulers in history, and as it often has in Anglo-American history. The uses and abuses of power depend upon culture as well as human nature.

More pertinent in our age of power, no doubt, is the truth of Lord Acton's observation. But the unprecedented power that men now command, the plainest threat to our civilization, brings up the plainest objection to the grand laws of Brooks Adams, Spengler, Toynbee, and the like. Those laws ultimately rest on arguments by analogy. They make some sense because of basic similarities in social need and response throughout history: broadly considered, history does repeat itself, most obviously in the familiar cycle of growth and decay, or rise and fall. Yet the great societies have all been dissimilar as well, the cycles never identical or neat; and in all history there is no real analogy to our present situation. Modern science and technology have produced an industrial society based on the machine. It is unique. So is large-scale democracy, with free education for all citizens. So is the extraordinary effort to create a United Nations, made possible by our technology and our knowledge of the entire world. By contrast with our civilization, the great Roman Empire was a provincial little hand-to-mouth affair. We may still learn something from its fate—we have the advantage of such knowledge, too—and we might share its fate, on a much grander catastrophic scale. Nevertheless there is no historical basis for Spengler's argument that we are *bound* to share it, or for Toynbee's argument that we can escape it only by praying to a God who failed to save the Roman Empire.

For the same reason history cannot tell us how to live with hydrogen bombs and sputniks, or how to build One World: men in the past never faced such problems. At this point history only gives us some warnings, tells us what to look out for. It may drive home the depressing platitudes about the corruptions of power and the besetting sins of self-righteousness; and doubtless this is the lesson men most need to learn. Yet even this is not simple. If human conflict always involves the ancient evils of selfishness and greed, it is usually intensified because both sides sincerely believe in the rightness of their cause and cannot understand the other side. The real tragedy of human existence, Hegel said, is the conflict not between right and wrong but between right and right. More precisely, I should say, the conflict is between men who, on both sides, are partly right and almost wholly self-righteous. Finally, Herbert Butterfield adds, we are face to face with the "absolute predicament and the irreducible dilemma"—the deadlocks that cannot be broken by sitting down around a table, any more than Catholicism and Protestantism have been able to reconcile their differences after centuries of discussion. We can only hope that men will somehow agree to live and let live, as Catholics and Protestants finally did after a century of atrocious religious wars; but the trouble is that when men are most fervent in their faiths, they are most likely to go to war.

10

# Oswald Spengler

## *predicted the West's decline*

*Peter Blume's* The Eternal City *looks as though it had been painted to a text from Oswald Spengler. It was not; it was simply one young American's reaction to Mussolini's Italy. But it epitomizes with stunning impact one of the final stages in the German historian's schedule of cultural decline and death: a time of ossified institutions, vulgar new Caesars, and manipulation of the mob.*

In the years of disillusion following World War I a great many people thought they had discovered a major prophet in Spengler, who seemed to echo and justify their own defeatism. They sought revelation in the pages of The Decline of the West, and found it in his melancholy prediction that Western civilization would be dead by A.D. 2200. The possibility is all too apparent — but few historians today would accept the deterministic theory of history by which Spengler arrived at his date. Cultures, he decided, live and die like any other organism: they all have roughly the same life span (*1,000 years*), and pass through an identical sequence of well-defined phases. He did not call these phases youth, maturity, and old age, but chose instead the seasons: spring, summer, autumn, winter.

There was nothing new in this notion; the idea is obvious and it had occurred to many historians before Spengler. What was new was the Teutonic thoroughness with which he worked it out. For him, the first three "seasons" are the growing, fruitful stages of a culture; winter is the moment when all is frozen into rigidity, when a culture becomes "complete" (his word). It is the end of the line.

The West, Spengler thought, was well into its winter months. He saw on every side the symptoms that he decided had marked the final stages of other cultures: the growth of monstrous cities, contention among empires, the rise of dictators, a political atmosphere of "Caesarism," and rule by "mobocracy" —all the things summarized with such virtuosity in Blume's painting.

Other cultures, when they died, have been reborn in the ones that succeeded them. But Oswald Spengler held out no such hope for the West: ours, he thought, would just dry up.

11

There remains a final paradox. The growth of an immense collective power, beyond the wildest dreams of men in the past, has made the individual liable to feel more impotent than ever before, and thus to conclude that man is now at the mercy of massive forces beyond his understanding and control. A more appalling thought is that this immense power is effectively at the disposal of a few individuals, in particular the leaders of America as well as Russia, who have secret information denied the rest of us. Upon decisions made by these very few depends the fate of our civilization. Any strictly deterministic theory of history founders on this fact; but so may the human race.

All this is to say that "history shows" a great deal more, and somewhat less, than men usually declare when they use this phrase. For those who do not pretend to know the one true interpretation of the great Bible it poses the problem of selection and emphasis. History is a record of all the great achievements of man, and of his repeated failures. It can make dismal reading, not only because all the civilizations before our own ended in failure, but because the causes of the failures are generally plainer than the causes of the creative achievements. Stupidity and folly are easier to understand than genius. The dark meanings of history are perhaps those that most need to be emphasized in the national forum, or in those business, political, and journalistic circles that boast of a purely material progress, glossed over with endorsements of moral and spiritual crusades that go about as deep as the testimonials used in advertising. (So most Americans applaud when their earnest President condemns the materialism of the Soviet.) For the more thoughtful, however, I judge that there is more need of countering the fashions in darkness, of risking sententiousness by dwelling on the creative achievements of man and in particular on the values of our own civilization. These might hearten us at a time when sanity and resolution seem as necessary as the religious faith that many say is our only hope of salvation. They are likely to be overlooked because they are a heritage we take for granted, the kind of thing that "goes without saying" and therefore without thinking.

Since we hear so much about the failure of science, of rationalism, of democracy, of our whole civilization, let us be really humble—even humbler than the specialists in humility. Christianity too is a failure by such standards—most clearly by its own standards. So have been the creeds by which all other societies lived and died in the past. But then we can add, in humility, that none of them completely failed in so far as they produced works that still live, ideals that men still cherish. In our immense and largely unconscious heritage we can point to all the lasting good that has come out of the historic failures. We can set realistic terms of historical judgment: partial successes, relative goods, mixed fruits. In these terms history does indeed show a progress, cultural and spiritual as well as material.

Today, to be sure, one must contemplate with some irony the verdict of Gibbon in *The Decline and Fall of the Roman Empire:* "We may therefore acquiesce in the pleasing conclusion that every age of the world has increased, and still increases, the real wealth, the happiness, the knowledge, and perhaps the virtue, of the human race." History certainly shows nothing so pleasing as a steady progress, with every age successively better than its predecessor. But just as certainly there has been an immense increase in knowledge; and all of us who read and write books must believe—in our hearts *do* believe—that knowledge does increase the real wealth of the human race and has some connection with its happiness, possibly even its virtue. It points to the wealth of values that man has realized and retained in spite of his repeated failures: skills and arts, ideas and ideals, including "higher" religions whose devotees may now condemn the faith in progress as sinful pride. In Western history it points to the political, intellectual, and religious freedoms that are no less cherished by most of these devotees, but were realized only in recent centuries. And a major inspiration to the effort to realize them, and extend them to ordinary men, was precisely the distinctive Western faith in progress stated by Gibbon. No such statement as his can be found, to my knowledge, in the whole literature of the world before his age.

The *will* to progress stimulated by this novel idea has been most apparent in America, a "land of opportunity" in which millions have worked to give their children better opportunities than they themselves enjoyed. Their hopeful spirit was not simply "human nature," for the peasant masses in all civilizations before our own accepted poverty as the law of life or the will of God. This suggests another reason why we cannot predict the future with certainty: prediction itself—that is, belief about the probable future—may make an incalculable difference in it. Marx's prediction that capitalism is inevitably doomed has helped to inspire a mighty effort to bring about that doom. It has also inspired efforts to reform capitalism and to control economic forces. Hence the free-for-all private enterprise system that Marx described, that Moscow still says is bound to wreck us and that conservatives say can alone save us, has long since ceased to exist. For such reasons the fate of a free society is bound up with the very hope of progress, or the despair of it.

"Realists" are now harping on a proverbial refrain: You can't change human nature. Those who insist that human nature is always the same always mean that man is naturally pretty bad, if not literally cursed by original sin; and given the long record of bloody failures, all history might appear to be on their side. Still, in a broad view of the evolution and the remarkable diversity of cultures that man has developed, one might be impressed more by the plasticity of his nature. Granted what any sensible man knows, that he is always frail and fallible and prone to unoriginal kinds of sin, the doctrine of original sin does not help much in understanding him, any more than it apparently has in getting

CONTINUED ON PAGE 128

# Arnold Toynbee
## looks for a universal church

The brooding face above stares at us from the apse of the church of San Vitale in Ravenna. It is a mosaic portrait of Archbishop Ecclesius, who holds, like an exquisite toy, a model of the church itself. It was under his auspices that San Vitale was begun in A.D. 526, just as the Roman Empire was finally breaking up. But we need not know these details of history to recognize in this image a symbol of the all-pervading influence of a "higher religion" and a "universal church." These terms come from Arnold Toynbee, who uses them to describe the final products of a disintegrating civilization. In A Study of History Toynbee brusquely rejects the blind determinism of Spengler, and says that "societies are not in any sense living organisms." But he does see a pattern in history, and it is even more elaborate than Spengler's. Civilization, for Toynbee, is the fruit of adversity, a successful response to a difficult challenge: harsh climate, poor soil. Success generates its own challenge, which—in a growing society—calls forth another successful response. But sooner or later a challenge comes along that is not met, and a breakdown occurs. Here begins a rhythmic sequence of "rout and rally." The end is death, or always has been, but before the final rout the stricken society produces a "universal state." It also produces a "universal church." In the death throes of the Hellenic society, whose universal state was the Roman Empire, Christianity was born. And what of us? Toynbee's message is obscure. For the emergence of a new or revived universal church, which in his scheme has always preceded extinction, now seems to him the West's one hope of avoiding it.

13

Steadily for two months I have been reading the work of some very new American writers, those in their twenties or a little past thirty who have recently published their first novels. Most of the writers belong to the first generation that is too young to have more than faint memories of the Depression, too young to have served in World War II, and just old enough to include the finished products of a new educational system. The generation used to be called Silent, but it has broken the silence, and its members are beginning to speak for themselves at a very early age. One of last season's novels, *The Fume of Poppies*, was written when the author was twenty years old and a senior at Harvard. One of this season's novels, praised by those who have seen it in manuscript, was written when the author, now a freshman, was only seventeen.

Given a chance to read it, I might have added another dimension to my report, which is now based on ten American first novels published in 1958. The choice was somewhat arbitrary, since I passed over some promising books that seemed to me outside the prevailing current. Other critics may have a different picture of the current. But all the novels discussed were praised or at least tolerated by reviewers, all are written with professional competence—or something more than that—and all have honesty enough to make them exist as books in themselves, not as mere indications of a prevailing fashion. What are their other characteristics as fiction and as commentaries on the completely new America in which the novelists are living?

As commentaries they are notable chiefly for what they omit. They start by omitting almost any mention of political ideas or political behavior on any level from that of village squabbles to that of nations in conflict. The fact is that the ten novels contain very few ideas of any sort, and those few are such innocuous notions as, for example, that a young man can get into trouble by trying to keep out of it. "I hate ideas," one hero says candidly. I doubt that the novelists hate ideas, but they must have been taught that novels are not the proper place in which to express them.

There is only a hint of social protest in these novels. How could there be more than a hint when the authors do not even try to offer a picture of society? The only social unit that most of them present is either what sociologists call the restricted family, consisting of husband, wife, and growing children, or else it is a little group of male and female tosspots who congregate in a special bar-and-grill. Only two attempts are made to present a somewhat larger community. *Home from the Hill*, by William Humphrey, portrays a county seat in East Texas as it was twenty years ago. *The Hard Blue Sky*, by Shirley Ann Grau, deals with a village of Cajun fishermen on a hurricane-wracked island in the Gulf of Mexico. These are two of the best novels by younger writers, and they merely add a qualification to the rule that applies to the others. When one of our younger novelists does try to present a community, he has to find it either in the past, as William Humphrey does, or on the outer margin of the American continent, as in the case of Miss Grau.

By MALCOLM COWLEY

# Ten authors in pursuit of one

*Such favorite themes of elder novelists as moral predicaments, social conflict, and political injustice are alien to this group of gifted young Americans, whose recent first novels are all preoccupied with sex — sometimes in the raw. To its eternal triangles they have added remarkable variations.*

Because the novels do not picture a society, they cannot deal with the old theme of rising or falling in society, that has played such a large part in American fiction on every level. It is often called the Horatio Alger story when the hero rises from poverty; but the protagonist may be a woman, and she may fall from a high position, as in Edith Wharton's best novel, *The House of Mirth*. In the books by younger writers nobody falls very far, and if anyone falls a short distance, the reason is not social prejudice but personal weakness. If a character rises in the financial scale, it is usually because of qualities such as selfishness, treacherousness, and hypocrisy. The Horatio Alger young man has become an American villain of the 1950's, if we still have villains.

Villains are almost completely absent from the novels under consideration, for the simple reason that the authors have no scale by which to measure villainy or virtue. Having been brought up permissively, they feel that anything is permitted, so long as it doesn't cause too much pain to other persons. The seven deadly sins aren't deadly in these novels; they aren't even sins. Pride, covetousness, lust, anger, gluttony, envy, and sloth are merely forms of behavior—permissible for the moment and in moderation, but perhaps leading to personal insecurity if carried too far. Even crimes that are listed in the penal statutes—theft, perjury, adultery, unnatural sexual connections, and murder—are represented as not being crimes in the true sense, but simply errors in conduct resulting from personal mal-

adjustment. The thief was deprived of love during his childhood, and so he "takes things" to give himself a sense of security. The murderer is in need of psychiatric care. By abandoning the notion of sin and atonement, the novelist loses a whole range of values on which fiction used to depend. If Hester Prynne, the heroine of *The Scarlet Letter*, was guilty of no real sin, why should she spend the rest of her life in expiation of that nothing? Why should the Reverend Arthur Dimmesdale climb to the scaffold of the pillory and, facing the Boston crowd, tear away the ministerial band from his breast to show that the letter *A* was imprinted in scarlet on his flesh? How can a novelist write another *Crime and Punishment* when he does not believe in punishment or crime?

One of the feelings expressed or implied in many of these novels is an indifference verging on apathy. The heroes and heroines have been privileged children, brought up by understanding parents, but it seems they have never done what they really wanted to do—chiefly because they didn't want it hard enough—and now they don't see why they should do anything at all except play it safe and have a good time. I said "heroes and heroines," but perhaps the young women should be omitted. Stronger because simpler than the men, they know what they want to do: make themselves loved, or a better word might be "desired." Most of them want to get married and have desirable children, and they move toward their goals like water seeking its level. It is the men who are cautious, apathetic, and

# subject

J. P. Donleavy

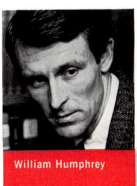

William Humphrey

Terry Southern

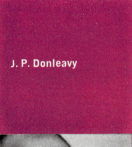

Richard Frede

Jonathan Kozol

Bianca Van Orden

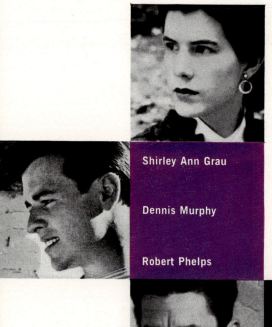

Shirley Ann Grau

Dennis Murphy

Robert Phelps

George P. Elliott

—since they reject involvement—likely to be overwhelmed.

Perhaps the best expression of this feeling is in *Entry E*, a novel by a recent Yale graduate named Richard Frede. The hero is a Yale junior who doesn't worry about being on probation and who lets himself "be talked into spending his afternoons and evenings dispassionately playing cards and seeing movies and talking and drinking. It was the weather, he supposed—dispassionately." One evening, however, Bogard finds himself confronted with the sudden need for making a moral decision.

It is the evening after the Princeton game. The students across the hall have been entertaining a girl from New York, a pathetic little tramp named Diana-Sue. They have decided to get her drunk and go to bed with her, all six of them and Bogard too, if he wants to be one of the gang. When they explain their plans to Diana-Sue, she thinks they are joking—but if they turn out to be serious, she isn't sure that she won't go along with them just for the hell of it. Bogard knows they are serious and tries to interfere with their plans, in a dispassionate fashion. He fights the ringleader, but doesn't fight hard enough to win. He asks other students in Entry E to save the drunken girl, but he doesn't persuade them to help. He even thinks of telephoning the campus police, but dismisses the idea; he doesn't want to be regarded as a rat. In the end all he does is help Diana-Sue into her clothes, after the gang has left, and put her on the train for New York.

When the college administration learns what has happened, as it was certain to do, the whole group of students is expelled—except Bogard, who is permitted to resign and come back the following year. Before leaving he has a talk with the dean, and it leads to one of the few social generalities expressed in any of these novels. "Each generation," the dean tells him, "gets known and tagged according to one small group within it. This group is the most influentially divergent group. In the twenties it was the expatriates and the young *nouveaux riches*—the *Lost* Generation. But they weren't the whole generation. Not even a significant part of it numerically. . . . Since the war—since the veterans' classes—I've been rather troubled by *your* generation . . . by those among the various classes who are going to shape and direct and characterize your generation. What do you think is their distinguishing characteristic?" Bogard doesn't know, and the dean answers his own question. "Indifference," he says. "An inability to get emotionally involved in anything. . . . The Indifferent Generation."

But this inability or unwillingness to feel anything deeply is only part of the picture. Most of the novels also express a rebellion against apathy and conformity, although the rebellion is never political. Always it is a personal or even trivial matter; sometimes it takes the mild form of not going back to college after the Christmas vacation. Many of the leading characters come from rich suburbs like Greenwich, Quaker Heights (in two novels), or Lake Forest, and

PHOTOGRAPHS BY DOROTHY HUMPHREY, GADIOT, KOBY, ALBURTUS, PHYLLIS CERF, ELLIOTT ERWITT, REBECCA LEPKOFF, STANLEY W. GOLD, BUNNY ADLER

their darkest fear is of being imprisoned for life in another suburb. The characters regarded as being heroic are those who escape the suburban habit of mind by doing whatever they want to do, at any cost to their financial prospects.

Usually they want to get happily drunk, go to bed with pretty girls, drive fast cars, and lead the life of semiadult delinquents. Paul Kyfe, the only admired character in *Entry E*, has a more innocuous ambition: he wants to ski all winter. He leaves Yale the Christmas of his sophomore year to become, in his own words, "a ski bum, a beach bum, a resort bum." "*Good God, man!* wake up!" he tells his friend Bogard. "You've got to do the things you *want* to do. That's the only way you'll outgrow 'em if they actually *do* need to be outgrown." The bull-chested hero of *The Ginger Man*, by J. P. Donleavy, has no intention of outgrowing his antisocial activities. He is an American married to a proper Englishwoman and studying, or pretending to study, at Trinity College in Dublin. He has no income except his monthly check under the GI Bill of Rights, but he is waiting for his father to die and leave him a fortune. Meanwhile he cheats the shopkeepers, swindles the landlord, smashes the furniture, deceives his wife, and takes money from a collection of mistresses; he even drinks his baby's milk each morning, so that the child becomes rachitic. The author presents his delinquencies with a sort of admiring wonder, as if he were describing the wreckage left behind by a tidal wave.

The hero of Jonathan Kozol's novel *The Fume of Poppies* is less admired and is even punished. He has left Harvard and run away to Europe with a beautiful Radcliffe girl, but his rebellion lasts only as long as his money. His weakness is "thinking you could escape a system, and then finding out it had hold of you all along, and feeling it pull you back." The end of the novel is funnier than the author intended it to be. During the voyage home the hero declines into apathy, while Wendy, his Radcliffe mistress, grows coarser and more aggressive. There is a last drunken night when Wendy deceives him with two men. One is a fifty-year-old Greek shipowner, "awfully solid and good about the things he did," but the other is a crew-cut Princetonian, and for that she can never be forgiven by the hero or, one suspects, by the author. Wendy and the hero separate, after an exchange of used-to-be-unprintable epithets, and she finds work in New York as a fashion model. The hero goes back to Harvard.

There is a final chapter in which one feels that the author is groping, as if at night in a quarry, for something to end the story with a tragic bang. At last he finds the bang: Wendy and the hero are going to get *married*. Not only that, but his father is giving him a job in an insurance agency, and the young couple will live in Wellesley Hills, in a ranch house.

I was tempted to say that these novels had no subjects, properly speaking—at least not in the sense that *War and Peace* has a subject, named in the title, and *Moby Dick* has a subject, which is whaling (as opposed to its theme, which is Captain Ahab's crazy search for the white whale), and any novel by Dickens or Balzac has a subject of its own. Henry James's novels have less specificity, but still there is a subject in the body of his work: the contrast between Americans and Europeans as representatives of a new and an old society. But since there is no society in most of these novels by younger authors, what do they find to write *about?* It took me a long time to see that there was an obvious answer to the question; the obvious is what we usually overlook. The new novels do have a general subject, as opposed to their particular themes; they even have two subjects, one minor and the other major. The minor subject, appearing in about half the novels, is driving automobiles fast; the major subject, appearing in all of them, is Sex.

I doubt whether the choice of subjects indicates a fundamental change in social customs. More Americans are driving automobiles more miles per year and hour than ever before, but there is no proof that more of them, proportionally, are being sexually promiscuous. If characters in the novels are almost all promiscuous, I suspect that is more the result of literary tendencies than it is a report on the social situation. Young novelists have been told by teachers and critics that they should present persons, not opinions. They have been told that politics is for journalists, society for sociologists, psychology for psychiatrists, and history for historians. Therefore they seize on what seems to be the only remaining field of study, that of interpersonal relations, and in this field they think that sex is the subject of broadest interest. They are also conscious of the fact that standards of proper expression have been relaxed, and that sexual behavior can now be presented in language that was unprintable ten years ago. A new territory seems to be open for fictional settlement, and they rush forward in a body as if to claim government homesteads in the Cherokee Strip.

There is a close connection between the minor and the major subject of the new fiction. Automobiles are described in terms that reveal the sexual personalities of their drivers. Thus, in *Parktilden Village*, by George P. Elliott, the principal character is a sociologist, and he drives a Buick convertible fresh from Detroit. Both car and owner are chromium-plated, full of mechanical devices, and lacking in human warmth. In *Heroes and Orators*, by Robert Phelps, the narrator's aggressively masculine cousin has a battered pickup truck in which he drives recklessly over the winding Catskill roads. Often there is a new girl on the seat beside him, and she is thrilled by her contact with unwashed and somewhat battered maleness. In *Flash and Filigree*, a comic fantasy by Terry Southern, there are two principal characters. One is a famous dermatologist, head of a clinic in Los Angeles, whose sexual passion is lavished on foreign sports cars. The

CONTINUED ON PAGE 117

17

# THE WORLD'S MOST

*Pier Luigi Nervi spans huge spaces*

*with light, airy concrete shells.*

*Now disciples are bringing the Italian's*

*graceful art to the Americas*

The most audacious and inventive designer of buildings today, who may well be the creator of a new architecture — an architecture totally liberated from preindustrial methods of construction—is by paradox not an architect at all. The Italian Pier Luigi Nervi is an engineer; and his breath-taking structures in reinforced concrete, which he calls "coverings," are by definition works of engineering. For they are calculated to perform their function, which is to span great areas of space, with maximum structural efficiency. Yet their incalculable coefficient is beauty. As an engineer, Nervi is a scientist. As a practical builder, he also heads an Italian construction firm. But in temperament he is, above all, an artist. More than any contemporary architect, not excepting Frank Lloyd Wright, he deserves the long-forgotten medieval title of master builder.

18

*The idea of bridging and economically enclosing wide spaces seized Nervi as a rising engineer. One of his revolutionary designs was for a series of wartime Italian Air Force hangars, one of which is shown here while under construction. No steel framework was used; the roof is simply a latticework of concrete beams designed to support thin sheeting and so attain challenging beauty.*

# DARING BUILDER

*By* ALLAN TEMKO

Nervi in truth is the most recent, and possibly the greatest, in the line of forthright engineers who have brought the Industrial Revolution to the art of building. This they have done almost against the will of architects. During the nineteenth century, architecture became a battle of styles. Neo-Gothic contended with Neo-Classic, Moorish with "Queen Anne," Flemish with Chinese and Ancient Egyptian. The architect was primarily a decorator who applied ornamentation to buildings that, beneath their frills, were boxes of inert masonry. But as architecture—or what the schools called architecture—thus descended to an unprecedented level of falseness, engineers such as Roebling in the United States and Eiffel in France were creating the significant monuments of the age. Their bridges, towers, stations, factories, and warehouses, in which the structural

forces at work were frankly, even proudly, revealed, marked the beginning of a new era not only in techniques but in aesthetics.

In their utilitarian structures the engineers also employed new materials of unprecedented strength: steel and, perhaps even more revolutionary, reinforced concrete. No one in the nineteenth century dreamed of the full possibilities of reinforced concrete, but ultimately, as in Nervi's work, it was to give free rein to man's structural imagination.

Concrete itself, of course, is hardly a "new" material. As early as 2800 B.C. the Egyptians used natural cement, composed of burnt gypsum and limestone, in the Sphinx. The Romans accomplished stupendous feats of construction with concrete, employing it in the immense dome of the Pantheon. But the use of concrete declined during the Middle Ages,

19

ILLUSTRATIONS FROM *The Works of Pier Luigi Nervi*; FREDERICK A. PRAEGER INC.

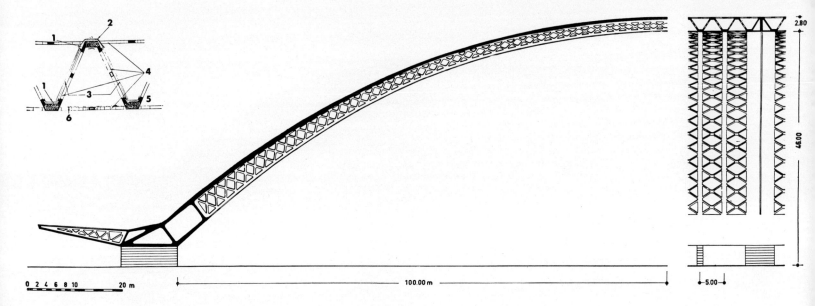

and during the Renaissance it vanished from architecture.

Centuries passed before it reappeared, not as a natural, but as a manufactured chemical product. In 1824 Portland cement—so called because of its superficial resemblance to white Portland stone—was patented by Joseph Aspdin, a Leeds bricklayer. The succeeding generation of British and French inventors considerably increased the strength of Portland cement, and by the 1850's a number of experiments in the reinforcement of concrete took place.

Reinforcement is necessary because concrete, unassisted by metal, has a particular shortcoming. Under compression —that is, under direct pressure—it has substantially the resistance of rock. But in bending, as internal stresses develop, it easily cracks and breaks. If steel, however, is appropriately placed within concrete, a *new* material is created. In Nervi's phrase, concrete then becomes "melted stone": a strangely wonderful stone which can be molded in any desired shape, and yet called upon to perform any structural task, for it simultaneously possesses the plasticity of concrete and the unrivaled strength of steel. As the num-

ber of buildings in reinforced concrete increased in Europe and the United States during the second half of the nineteenth century, a deeper understanding of the material's properties developed. Finally, in 1889, the great French engineer Paul Cottancin obtained a patent for a complete system of reinforced concrete construction. Two years later Nervi was born at Sondrio in the Italian Alps.

Merely to be born in Italy is to be assured of a liberal architectural education. The play of light on colored surfaces; the calm grandeur of a dome, or the militant form of a tower, dominating a town; the human spontaneity of medieval squares; the energy of fountains; the sudden opening of vistas of baroque space: all are part of any Italian's life. To an Italian as sensitive as the young Nervi, the past was not a textbook to be ransacked for picturesque details. It was a vast, brilliant classroom, filled with luminous space, in which he was taught by masters as incomparable as Brunelleschi. Nervi studied the dome of the Florence cathedral as it should be studied, as a living example of intrepid structural courage. Brunelleschi, aided only by empirical knowledge and practical experience, was forced to grapple with problems that today can be solved in a few minutes with the aid of a slide rule. But, as Nervi enjoys pointing out, no amount of mathematics, however accurate, will enable a man to erect Florence's dome.

Nervi's name, which literally means "nerves," evokes with singular accuracy his restless, searching intellect and his hatred of formal doctrine. A curious incident occurred in 1913, during his last year as an engineering student at the University of Bologna, which confirmed his distrust of textbook architecture. François Hennebique, another of the French engineers who did much of the pioneering work in reinforced concrete, had designed the Risorgimento bridge in Rome. Nervi's teacher of structures—fortunately, one of the few academicians who did grasp the limitations of existing theoretical knowledge—read to the class letters from

JANE DOGGETT

*Pier Luigi Nervi*

alarmed professors in Germany, who proved mathematically that the daring concrete bridge would fail. If it were built, they demonstrated, it would surely fall. But the bridge, slenderly spanning the Tiber, already stood completed and was bearing its daily load of heavy traffic, as it still does.

More impressive than the work of Hennebique was that of his ingenious Swiss friend Robert Maillart. Across the Alpine gorges early in the century, Maillart launched his first exquisite bridges of reinforced concrete. These spans, daringly conceived and executed, were structurally alive to their last millimeter, curving above ribbonlike arches, mastering space without the slightest suggestion of strain.

Then came the First World War. Nervi served as a lieutenant in the engineers and worked on commonplace military installations. He did not have the good fortune of the French engineer Eugène Freyssinet, who was assigned to build two hangars for dirigibles at Orly. These tremendous corrugated parabolic shells—each spanned 320 feet—were the first of their kind, and owed their remarkable strength, as did Maillart's bridges, to design alone. A quarter of a

TEXT CONTINUED ON PAGE 24

*The new ideas demonstrated in Nervi's hangars were carried further in the wartime design (above) for a railroad station hall 660 feet wide, roofed with prefabricated reinforced concrete. Nervi's construction drawings (opposite) show (1) a section through the roof units, (2) a cross section of the vault, (3) a longitudinal section. The same concepts were realized in his huge 1949 exhibition hall at Turin.*

*Below left, movable forms are prepared for pouring supporting elements in an Italian factory, using Nervi's new ferro-cemento. The resulting design bears resemblance to the tracery executed in masonry in vaulted Gothic buildings. On the following two pages are other examples of the shapes and design motifs Nervi achieves with his use of economical materials handled in a revolutionary manner.*

PHOTOGRAPHS COURTESY OF ADA LOUISE HUXTABLE

21

OVERLEAF: 1 AND 4, G. E. KIDDER SMITH; 2, 3, 5, AND 6, COURTESY OF PIER LUIGI NERVI

1 Exhibition Hall, Turin (1949)

2 Palazzetto dello Sport, Rome (1958)

3 Stadio Flaminio, Rome (1958)

4 Exhibition Hall, Turin (1949)

5 Health resort, Chianciano (1952)

6 Tobacco Factory, Bologna (1952)

TEXT CONTINUED FROM PAGE 21

century later, when Nervi was designing his great exposition hall at Turin, he was to draw direct inspiration from them.

After the war Nervi went to work for a construction company in Rome. But the work, which seemed to him hopelessly conservative, soon became intolerable. He opened his own office, only to find that few contractors would bid on his designs. So he decided, as Maillart, Hennebique, and other innovators had before him, to go into the construction business too. At last, in 1926, when he was thirty-five years old, he began construction of the Cinema Augusteo in Naples.

This comparatively small circular auditorium (one hundred feet in diameter) received little attention at the time, for more important work was being accomplished elsewhere, especially by German architects. But structurally it was prophetic of things to come. The balcony spans the width of the hall without intermediate supports of any kind. The roof was the first of Nervi's "coverings." Like a wheel, its frame fans outward from an open ring that serves as the hub. From rim to rim the wheel, filled completely with glass, measures sixty-five feet across, resembling a great rose window of the Middle Ages turned on its side. It was the earliest of Nervi's "flowers," which were to grow more delicate with time.

Steel, of course, could have done the same job, probably with as much elegance or more; but in Italy, where steel is scarce, concrete was readily available and—something Nervi has never failed to take into account—much cheaper.

Economy, he has found again and again, is a powerful aesthetic factor in the new architecture. "In the absence of good taste," he declares, low cost "is the best incentive for art" that exists among his clients. Virtually all of his commissions have been awarded on the basis of competitive bidding. Nervi the designer, inseparable from Nervi the contractor, has repeatedly underbid rivals with estimates so low as to seem scarcely credible. In 1929 he won the competition for a 35,000-seat stadium at Florence not because its design was to cause an artistic sensation, but because its cost of only $2.90 per place would enable the structure to pay for itself in a few afternoons. There has never been a more monumental bargain.

Around a playing field 660 feet long—almost twice the length of an American football field—Nervi erected stands which basically are continuous flights of steps. The steps serve both as beams and seats, and are supported at intervals by rising diagonal braces, which in turn are mounted on pillars. At the turns on either end, the structure rises clear of the ground on a series of powerful buttresses. An extraordinary roof is cantilevered seventy-five feet into space above the main grandstand, providing shelter from sun or rain without marring the unobstructed view of the field. Equally extraordinary are the six exterior staircases, which Nervi suspended in thin air, each consisting of two intertwined spirals of concrete, boldly projecting from the structure.

The Florence stadium, completed in 1932, made Nervi famous. Nevertheless three years elapsed before he received another major commission. In the meantime he drew up plans for several fascinating projects that, unfortunately, were never built. One was a bridge, carried by gigantic A-frames, across the Biedano Valley near Rome. Another was a double-decked stadium, designed to provide unobstructed visibility for 100,000 spectators and to be evacuated in twelve minutes.

Then, after a competition held in 1935 by the Italian Air Force, Nervi was awarded a commission to build a series of hangars that were to exert a profound influence on architecture. The hangars presented exceptionally difficult problems. First of all, the structures were to be immense: 330 by 130 feet. To vault such an area without intermediate supports is a prodigious feat. One cannot simply adapt a design that proved satisfactory in a smaller structure; an entirely new structural system must be devised. (If the human body, to give an analogy, were increased ten times in size, the bone structure and the nervous, respiratory, and circulatory systems would have to be radically changed.) Not only did Nervi face this problem of immense size, but he was also confronted, as might be expected, by the need for the most stringent economy in money and materials. Italy was already at war with Ethiopia, and structural steel and lumber for formwork were very scarce.

The hangars were erected at different places in Italy in two main groups. The first group, for structures of such dimensions, displayed lightness and grace unprecedented in reinforced concrete construction. Nervi erected a lithe latticework of intersecting concrete beams, whose apertures were filled with asbestos-cement slabs over two-inch concrete to compose the roof. The immense structure seemed to float in the air. The numerous supports gave some indication of its mass. There were six buttresses on either

CONTINUED ON PAGE 121

*Nervi's example has influenced some of today's leading architects in the Western world. A particularly original adaptation of the uses of concrete shells is that of the Mexican Félix Candela in a restaurant at Xochimilco (center, opposite). The young American Minoru Yamasaki has also used thin-shelled concrete vaults in his St. Louis air terminal building (upper left), a building that won a First Honor Award from the American Institute of Architects in 1956, and in his new Parke-Davis building in Menlo Park, California, a model of which is shown at lower left. An especially large shell is that of the 1958 Palais des Expositions at Paris (upper right), designed by a team of architects including Bernard Zehrfuss, who worked with Nervi on the UNESCO building in Paris. At lower right, Harrison & Abramovitz's assembly hall at the University of Illinois is designed for both sports and meetings.*

24

MINORU YAMASAKI, ST. LOUIS AIR TERMINAL

NEW PALAIS DES EXPOSITIONS, PARIS

FÉLIX CANDELA, RESTAURANT IN XOCHIMILCO, MEXICO

YAMASAKI, BUILDING IN CALIFORNIA

HARRISON & ABRAMOVITZ, ASSEMBLY HALL

MARLENE ROTHKIN

*Gaius Julius Caesar, Supreme Commander, Dictator for the Fourth Time, Consul for the Fifth Time, Supreme Priest, Augur, to . . .*

*The Honorable Robert Moses, City Construction Co-ordinator of New York City, Member of the New York Planning Commission, Chairman of the Mayor's Slum Clearance Committee, President of the Bethpage Park Authority, President of the Jones Beach Parkway Authority, President of the Long Island State Park Commission, Commissioner of Parks of the City of New York, Chairman of the New York State Council of Parks, Chairman of the Triborough Bridge & Tunnel Authority, Chairman of the Power Authority of the State of New York:*

Greetings!

They tell me that of all men you wield greatest power over the streets, the parks, the public buildings of the greatest city in the world. I, too, was master of a great city, and I shall forego the question of which is the greater. Your New York is greater than . . . how many others? My Rome was not merely greater, there were no others. But I shall not dispute you.

You have caused great bridges to leap across the rivers which encircle your metropolis. You have demolished ruins and put modern structures in their place. For the populace you have built clean and commodious places of pleasure and amusement. Greatest of all are your highways, your smooth avenues, expeditious and graceful, which aid your city's citizens in the pursuit of their multifarious tasks and carry the unending flow of their traffic in and out, systole and diastole, like the beating of a great heart.

Who can imagine a city without its roads? Being builder of the roads, you are the true builder of the city, and being a Roman—for we had no small fame as builders—I can salute you. But most of all I address you as brother in your own unhappy task, one that I know to my anguish, of doing for the people that which is best for them despite their wishes.

Out to the boundaries of the known world I established peace. To the masses of mankind, often against their will, I extended the blessings of Roman law. I abolished torture; I corrected the calendar; I saw to it that the inhabitants of the empire did not starve, holding good years and harvests in the balance against bad. All of this I did, and more, and none of it stayed the bloody hands of my fellow Romans on the Ides of March.

That is another story. I am told that you too have begun to feel on the back of your head the burning eyes of public disaffection. To be master is to suffer, how much only we who have suffered thus may know. But when I look at your powers, your many offices, I marvel that you have not been able to cure a municipal disease that is as old as Rome—I mean the plague of traffic. And so, in your kindness, I

*By* ERIC LARRABEE

venture to offer certain advices on this agonizing matter.

The fate of a great city is to be the lodestar of man's desire. With an eternal fascination it draws unto itself more of humanity than it can decently house, feed, and satisfy. They say that in your city the crush of gaudy chariots is so great that a man may go faster on foot than by hiring a conveyance. This I am astonished that you permit.

We too had a traffic problem. We built roads unto the ends of the earth, and all of them led back to Rome. Down them came Cilicians, Cappadocians, Parthians, Germans, Nubians, Jews, Egyptians, Dacians, Arabians, Britons, Æthiopians, Sabaeans, Sarmatians, Sigambrians—all came to Rome.

Great were the spectacles that Rome offered her people, but greatest of all were her people themselves. In our cramped and crowded streets could be heard the babel of a hundred tongues. Here would be ambassadors from the Cimbri, Moorish slaves leading an elephant, the chanting priests of Isis in their linen robes.

In my time the crowd became too much to bear—beggars, peddlars, snake charmers, scholars, pickpockets, butchers, heavy beasts and creaking wagons, in a din of noise and shouting that continued day and night. Other men may complain of such matters, but Caesar must act. I did so. I resorted to extreme measures. I banned the wheeled vehicle from the center of the city.

In 46 B.C. I proclaimed the *Lex Julia municipalis*, a document of tedious detail, but I recall to you its essential passage: "In the roads which are or shall be within the city of Rome, within the limit of continuous habitation no person, after the first day of January next following, shall be allowed in the daytime, after sunrise or before the tenth hour of the day, to lead or drive any heavy wagon. . . ."

Of course I had to make exceptions. How foolish they are, do you not agree, who think that a dictator merely does what he pleases? I had to exempt religious ceremonies and triumphal parades, and processions for the circuses, and the necessary transport of materials for the sacred temples and other public works; but in the main I achieved my purpose. From dawn to dusk no wheeled vehicles came within the Urbs.

I had my way. My law survived me. Emperors came and went, but into the city came only the carts of building contractors. I made Imperial Rome unique, and with effortless ease she went on to absorb and rise above her various and conflicting elements, and become incomparable.

The secret of the great city is to let it breathe. I am sure that sooner or later you will discover this, but in the meantime—should milder answers fail—I commend to you my own example. The heart of the city is for man; bar the four-wheeled engines, restore it to him, and your children's children will rise up to bless your name.

*Vale.*

*In this sixteenth-century Persian miniature, Alexander appears as a Timurid horseman. The head on the facing page may be a Roman copy of a statue done by Leochares in Alexander's lifetime.*

# THE TWO WORLDS OF ALEXANDER

SOMEWHERE ALONG THE ROUTE OF HIS ASIAN CONQUESTS THE YOUNG HERO DISCOVERED A VISION OF WORLD UNITY WHICH FOREVER CHANGED THE DESTINIES OF WESTERN MEN

*By* C. A. ROBINSON, JR.

Alexander passed across Asia like a flash, and since he never lost a battle and was young, handsome, and personally dramatic, he stirred the imagination of men as few have ever done. He was, as Napoleon said, the greatest general who ever lived. But his real significance, in the history of Western civilization, goes beyond his military genius to his conception of a world state based on the equality and co-operation of all peoples. This political vision, so strangely found in a young and prideful conqueror, outlasted his life and his empire to inspire men in every age from his day to ours.

So dazzling was Alexander's military conquest that for centuries it almost obscured his real nature. In fact, medieval Europe and the Orient of all periods completely forgot the true Alexander. They knew only the Alexander of legend and romance, embedded in an amazing body of literature that began to form soon after his death and ultimately circulated, in eighty versions and in twenty-four languages, from Iceland to Malaya.

Even today chieftains in remote parts of Turkestan claim descent from Alexander, while their ordinary folk are said to be sprung from his soldiers and their horses from Bucephalus. The early Christians portrayed Jesus in Alexander's likeness, the Jews looked upon Alexander as a propagandist of the Most High, and the Koran calls him Dulcarnain, the Lord of Two Horns. Alexander, or Iskander as he has generally been known to Asia, was supposed to have built a gate to exclude Gog and Magog, who were later equated with the Ten Tribes of Israel and then with barbarism itself. As geographical knowledge expanded, the mythical gate was moved from the Caucasus to the Great Wall of China and finally to the Arctic Circle. Still other stories brought the conqueror of the known civilized world to the Blue Nile and to Britain—and then, as if that were not enough, to the heavens and on to the Land of Darkness and even farther to the end of the world, where one finds the Well of Life.

The net of legend extended back to include Alexander's father, King Philip of Macedon, and his mother, Olympias, an Epirote princess of fiery, passionate nature. Ancient historians, for example, say that Philip met this imaginative and terrible woman when both were initiated into the mysteries of Samothrace. During religious celebrations, it seems, Olympias was always more deeply affected than other women and used to supply the reveling companies with great tame serpents, which would often lift their heads from out of the ivy or coil themselves about the garlands of the women, thus terrifying the men. At any rate, according to the story, she and Philip fell in love with each other on sight.

Some time after their marriage, the story continues, Philip dreamed that he was putting a seal upon his wife's womb; and the device of the seal, as he thought, was the figure of a lion. Some seers said that Philip should keep a closer watch upon his young wife, but Aristander, the best of all seers, maintained that the woman was pregnant, since no seal was put upon what was empty, and pregnant with a son whose nature would be bold and lionlike.

Moreover, it was commonly believed in antiquity that the temple of Artemis at Ephesus burned to the ground on the night of Alexander's birth. One witness made a remark frigid enough to extinguish the flames, to the effect that it was little wonder that the temple had burned because the goddess was busy bringing Alexander into the world. Since the ancient Greeks loved coincidences, it is probable that they moved the month of Alexander's birth back to midsummer (356 B.C.) in order that Philip, who had just taken a large Greek city, might receive three messages simultaneously: that Parmenio, his chief general, had conquered the Illyrians in a great battle; that his race horse had won a victory at the Olympic games; and that Alexander III, as he was later called, had been born at Pella, the capital of Macedonia. The seers added to Philip's delight by saying that the son whose birth coincided with three victories would always be victorious.

Philip was a practical man and military genius with the savage appetites and passions of his mountaineer ancestors. For the sake of honor and renown, as his bitter Athenian opponent, the orator Demosthenes, declared, he was ready to let his eye be gouged out, his collarbone broken, his hand and his leg disabled. Personally ambitious, urbane, and friendly, Philip lacked moral scruples and was ready at any time to lie, to break a treaty, to buy friends, or to bribe statesmen. He seemed to feel that a diplomatic victory was as good as one on the battlefield, and he had the ability to lull states to a sense of security until the time arrived for striking the fatal blow. "Taken all in all," concluded a contemporary, "Europe has not yet produced such a man as Philip, the son of Amyntas."

It is a safe guess that Alexander inherited his military skill and cold rationalism from his father. But the son's own inner being, his mysticism and romanticism and impetuousness, came from his mother, Olympias. Perhaps from her, too, came the ability to kindle the imagination of multitudes by a single act—as when, desiring to rally the Greeks wholeheartedly to his cause at the outset of his expedition against the Persian Empire, he visited Troy and stirred in the breast of every Greek glorious memories and the picture of a new Trojan War against the Asiatic foe.

*T*he great structure of legend that grew up around the birth of Alexander finds reflection in this fifteenth-century French miniature. It was said that the air changed color, that thunder and lightning shook the earth, that animals shivered with fear and everything trembled at Alexander's birth because he would conquer and rule all things. It was said that wise men gathered to discuss the strange portents. It was said, too, that when Olympias delivered her baby, thirty other princes were born in Greece and surrounding countries—Alexander's future officers. Later it was even said that his father was not Philip of Macedon, whose image is shown on the contemporary coin at left, but the god Zeus.

31

*For three years, Aristotle (above) tutored Alexander and some of his companions at Mieza, near Pella. There they studied letters, including grammar, rhetoric, and dialectic; arithmetic, geometry, and astronomy; gymnastics, for Aristotle believed in the merits of a sound body as well as a trained mind; drawing and music. Alexander used to say that he loved Aristotle more than his father, for the one had given him life but the other had taught him the noble life. The relationship of Alexander and Aristotle gave medieval writers and artists an occasion to remind their fourteenth-century monarchs of the importance of encouraging scholarship and of surrounding themselves with learned men.*

At the age of thirteen, Alexander had the philosopher Aristotle as a teacher, and during three impressionable years his keen mind became thoroughly Greek in character, while his romantic imagination developed a love for Homer and his supposed ancestors Heracles and Achilles. On his expedition to Asia, Alexander took along a text of the *Iliad*, which Aristotle had edited for him, and kept it with his dagger under his pillow at night. It seems clear that Aristotle implanted in the youth a love of learning of encyclopedic scope, with a special interest in scientific investigation and medicine. Moreover, Alexander learned from the philosopher that moderation is necessary in government —a virtue he was not likely to get from Olympias—and he also learned, or rather was taught, that all barbarians (i.e., non-Greeks) were slaves by nature, especially those of Asia.

Alexander's admiration for Greek culture was tempered by the simple, vital, active life of Macedonia. This was a narrow coastal strip, with a mountainous interior, along the Aegean Sea in northern Greece. Though the Macedonians were Greeks, the proud citizens of Old Greece southward despised them as a semicivilized people with a veneer of Greek culture.

These Macedonians, who were destined to remake the world, formed the first nation in European history. Rough and simple though they were, they looked upon themselves as one people, and not, in Greek fashion, as the citizens of this city or that. In the time of Philip and Alexander, the Greeks themselves were caught up in a deep crisis. Were they to continue to insist on the sovereignty of their city-state, or had the time come for a fundamental change in their thinking, for a reconciliation of autonomy with a wider union? A century earlier, in the days of Periclean Athens, they had reached a summit of civilization never before attained by the human race. Now—despite great men such as Praxiteles, Plato, and Aristotle, who lived amongst them—they were torn by fratricidal warfare, an economic depression, and the interference by the Great King of the predatory Persian Empire in their internal affairs. How much attention, therefore, should they pay to certain orators who were urging them to unite under the Macedonian monarchy in a war against Persia, the traditional foe?

The sharp division in Greek thought exactly suited Philip's personal ambitions. By 338 B.C. he found that Athens and Thebes were the only city-states remaining that would fight effectively on behalf of Greek freedom. Without much difficulty he defeated them at Chaeronea in a battle that ended forever the ability of Greek city-states to dominate the peninsula's politics. And then he called together at Corinth representatives of most of the states in Greece and joined them in a federation known as the League of Corinth.

The chief action of the League was to appoint Philip commander in chief of a Panhellenic war of revenge against Persia, to punish her for her invasion of Greece a century and a half earlier. Doubtless, Philip planned no more than an expedition against Asia Minor, for the empire of the Persians stretched 2,700 miles from the Hellespont (or Dardanelles) across Asia Minor through Syria, Palestine, and Egypt, and then eastward through Mesopotamia and Iran to India. It was a rich and mighty state, well-governed and able to dispose large armies of disciplined, courageous men. In Asia Minor alone there were 20,000 superb Persian cavalry; and of the various other troops, 20,000 obstinate Greek mercenaries formed the empire's chief hope as heavy infantry.

Philip delayed his departure two years, during which time he gave himself alternately to state business and carousals. Then, suddenly, he was murdered. At the age of twenty, Alexander fell heir to his kingdom, his army, his plan of the Asiatic expedition, and the command of the Corinthian League.

If Alexander is famous for incredible speed of action, he should also be known for his caution at almost every point in his career. Instead of rashly setting off for Asia in what could only have been another in a long line of interminable wars, this youth spent the next two years insuring that his lines of communication would not be cut while he was absent from Greece. This required long marches through trackless forests, over high mountain ranges, and across the Danube to what is today Bulgaria, Rumania, and eastern Yugoslavia, striking such fear into the hearts of the inhabitants that they did not stir during his absence.

The expedition against Asia, when at last it was ready to set out, had an air of permanence about it. Artists, poets, philosophers, and historians went along with Alexander, just as in later days they were to accompany Napoleon. There were also surveyors and engineers, geographers, hydrographers, geologists, botanists, and other scientists to study the phenomena of Asia and perhaps to send back to Aristotle specimens for further observation. One person deserves special mention: Aristotle's nephew, the historian Callisthenes. He was implicated in a plot against Alexander's life in Central Asia, was arrested and executed. Aristotle hated Alexander for this, and so powerful was Aristotle's influence that, when the generation that knew Alexander died out, not a favorable biography of him was written for three centuries. Instead there was created the familiar picture of the bloodthirsty, lucky despot, which it has been the task of modern scholarship to study and correct.

Alexander's army of Macedonians and Greek allies consisted of about 30,000 infantry and 5,000 cavalry. These troops rarely fought as a body, but even when only small contingents were engaged, Alexander combined the various arms. This practice, and especially the close union of light troops and cavalry with the phalanx, largely explains the invincibility of the Macedonian military machine. Moreover, Alexander invariably pursued the enemy with the aim of destroying him utterly, a policy which the Prussian strategist Von Clausewitz has termed "the strategy of defeat."

In a pitched battle, Alexander's army was likely to line up as follows: in the center, intended as a firm anchor, was

*A*mid the flowering hills and mists of Delphi, the oracle proclaimed Alexander invincible. These prophetic words caused the young chosen Macedonian king to rejoice, for at twenty he was to lead his armies into the depths of lands yet unexplored by Europeans.

33

*S*traight *toward the Persian king, his lance piercing a foe, rides Alexander (left) at the Battle of Issus in 333* B.C. *Mounted on his horse, Bucephalus, Alexander wears a breastplate with the head of the mythical Medusa whose face had turned all who saw it to stone. Darius, standing high in his chariot, is distinguished by his tiara, the symbol of kingship.*

*In this damaged Roman mosaic, discovered as a pavement at the House of the Faun in Pompeii in 1831, the two kings are shown in much closer proximity than they actually ever were. The mosaic, which dates from the first century* A.D., *is a copy of a painting done by a contemporary of Alexander. The Romans became widely acquainted with the exploits of Alexander through the* Parallel Lives *of Plutarch who, as a Greek living within the Roman Empire, wanted to demonstrate that the Greeks had their full share of heroes long before Rome achieved its glory.*

the phalanx—9,000 heavily armed infantrymen, formed in a mobile rectangle eight or more men in depth, with three feet between every two men. This demanded soldiers who were highly trained and disciplined, who would not huddle together for safety, but it also meant that rough ground or momentary shocks from the enemy would not disarrange the mass. To the right of the phalanx came Alexander and his magnificent Companion cavalry—the real striking arm —with lancers, javelin men, and archers thrown out to their right as flankers and skirmishers. To the left were other cavalry and light troops. Parmenio, the second in command, was in charge of the left wing. As an able and cautious tactician he was especially suited for this post, since in the oblique order of battle (the favorite also of Frederick the Great of Prussia) it was the duty of the left wing to hold firm, while Alexander, choosing the decisive moment, charged from the right and rolled the enemy in upon the spears of his slowly advancing infantry.

Alexander varied these arrangements as circumstances dictated. As for tactics, he once said that this was merely a matter of using his brains; his success, he added, was due to never putting anything off. His men worshiped him, and though obviously he was not a reckless adventurer, they had no doubt about his lucky star.

35

Alexander's organizing ability manifested itself in the siege train, which was far superior to anything of its kind elsewhere. There were siege towers, placed on rollers or wheels and covered with hides to protect them from fires; they might be over 150 feet high, with many stories, so that the top of any part of an enemy wall could be reached. Boarding bridges were used at Tyre for the first time in history. It was possible to undermine the enemy's walls by tunneling or to knock them down with battering rams, which had huge beams over 100 feet long with metallic heads. The besiegers themselves were protected by movable sheds, known in later days as tortoises. But the greatest military invention of antiquity, used for the first time at Tyre by Alexander, was the torsion catapult, which could fire huge arrows accurately for 200 yards as well as stones weighing fifty or sixty pounds. Alexander never employed

catapults as field artillery in a pitched battle, but he used them in irregular warfare, in sieges, mounted on ships as at Tyre, and to clear a river's bank of the enemy.

Over this army, infused with a proud professional spirit, stood Alexander, commander in chief of the League of Corinth, and as king of Macedon responsible to no one but himself in military matters and (subject to certain checks of the army assembly) in civil affairs as well. By his side he had seven bodyguards, a staff of what we might describe as general officers, and also a group of eighty to one hundred influential officers, known simply as Companions. These men formed his council, as it were, and provided military and civil officers as needed.

The Grand Army was destined to march under Alexander many thousands of miles during eleven long years, often at terrific speed; it was not unusual for a contingent to cover

MAP BY DAVID GREENSPAN; DRAWINGS BY EMMA LANDAU

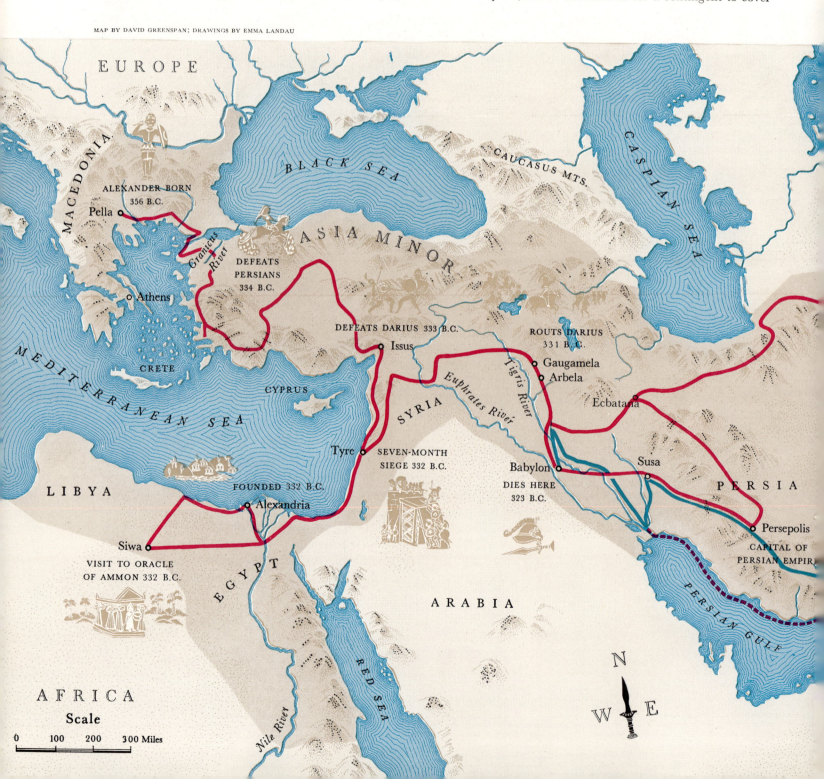

EUROPE

MACEDONIA

ALEXANDER BORN 356 B.C.
Pella

BLACK SEA

CAUCASUS MTS.

CASPIAN SEA

Granicus River

DEFEATS PERSIANS 334 B.C.

ASIA MINOR

Athens

DEFEATS DARIUS 333 B.C.

Issus

ROUTS DARIUS 331 B.C.

Gaugamela
Arbela

CRETE

CYPRUS

MEDITERRANEAN SEA

Euphrates River

Tigris River

Ecbatana

SYRIA

Tyre    SEVEN-MONTH SIEGE 332 B.C.

Babylon
DIES HERE 323 B.C.

Susa

PERSIA

LIBYA

FOUNDED 332 B.C.
Alexandria

Siwa

VISIT TO ORACLE OF AMMON 332 B.C.

EGYPT

ARABIA

Persepolis
CAPITAL OF PERSIAN EMPIRE

PERSIAN GULF

RED SEA

Nile River

N
W  E

AFRICA
Scale
0    100    200    300 Miles

forty or fifty miles a day with him for several days. Events frequently proved his bravery and self-discipline. He was often wounded—on the neck, head, shoulder, and in the thigh; in Turkestan, the fibula of his leg was broken; thrice he was wounded in Afghanistan; in India an arrow pierced his lung; and besides he suffered attacks of fever and dysentery. Every inch of the march was new, yet his reinforcements reached him regularly, over 60,000 in the first eight years alone. And every inch of the way he met opposition, save in Egypt. He fought four pitched battles: three with Persia, and another with an Indian rajah in the Punjab, where he encountered for the first time large numbers of terrifying elephants who barred his passage of a great river.

In addition to the disciplined armies of the ancient East, which greatly outnumbered his own, Alexander had also to fight fierce mountain tribes. There were deserts to overcome, and a long guerrilla warfare with its utterly strange tactics awaited him in eastern Iran. There were, too, strong cities to besiege, the island city of Tyre alone requiring seven months and all his tenacity.

Alexander's plan was probably to conquer as much of the Persian Empire as possible and hold on to it, but his every success opened up further vistas until the possession of the entire empire was his. The conquests confronted him with enormous problems of administration, for he now had an empire of his own that contained not only many different races but peoples in all stages of civilization. Greater still, since his ambitions developed in this direction, was the task of giving a sense of unity to a world state.

It was in the spring of 334 B.C. that Alexander, then twenty-two years of age, began the march. Many portents from heaven were reported; it was said, for example, that

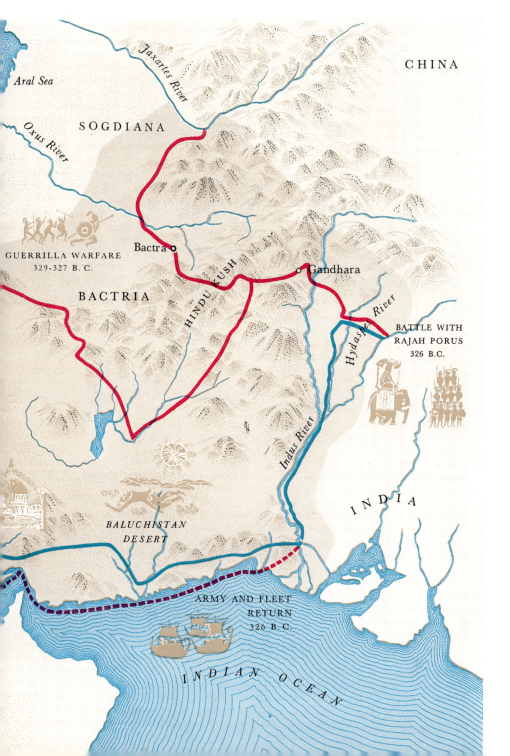

# THE ROUTE OF ALEXANDER

ROUTE OF MARCH

RETURN ROUTE

ROUTE OF NEARCHUS

*In The Family of Darius Before Alexander by Paolo Veronese, the painter bestowed upon the Macedonian the favorable verdict of the sixteenth-century Italian Renaissance scholars, who found in the newly translated editions of the Greek historians Arrian and Plutarch an Alexander of nobility and compassion. An elegant Venetian square surrounded by Palladian archways has here become the setting for the famous incident which followed the Battle of Issus. Darius' mother, Sisygambis, having first knelt before Hephaestion, thinking he was the King, has discovered her mistake and now turns in humiliation to Alexander. But the King, gesturing toward his friend, assures the Queen that Hephaestion too is Alexander. The conqueror's honorable treatment of Statira, Darius' wife, and the daughter Barsine, whom he later married, was the model of Renaissance social conduct extolled by Castiglione in The Courtier. "Have continence," he advised, "as did Alexander the Great towards the very beautiful women of Darius—an enemy and a vanquished one at that."*

the wooden statue of Orpheus sweated profusely. Most people feared the sign, but Aristander, the reliable seer, bade Alexander be of good cheer and assured him that he was to perform deeds worthy of song and story that would cost poets and musicians much toil and sweat to celebrate. Thus, amid great excitement, the army set out for Asia under a leader who was destined never to return.

Darius III, the Great King of Persia, considered it beneath his dignity to bother personally with yet one more intruder from Greece. This he left to his satraps in Asia Minor; but when they were decisively defeated at the Granicus River, **he** began to bestir himself and collected an army of perhaps 100,000 men. Alexander was now at Tarsus, with all of Asia Minor successfully behind him. He knew that Darius and his vast host were somewhere in the broad Syrian plains: he feigned sickness, hoping to entice

Darius into the narrow plain of Cilicia. This was the only time in his life that his intelligence service broke down, for it happened that either king tired of waiting for the other, and Alexander crossed the Amanus Mountains in search of Darius the very night that Darius crossed the same range by a different pass in search of him.

Alexander found himself with his lines of communication cut, a hostile empire all around him, and Darius between him and home. Immediately he retraced his steps and at Issus overwhelmed the Persians. Darius, who was a coward as well as a despot, promptly fled and despite the rapid pursuit managed to escape.

On his return to camp that night, Alexander found that his men had picked out for him the tent of Darius, which was full to overflowing with gorgeous servitors and many treasures. Straightway, then, according to Plutarch (the

biographer of the first century A.D.), Alexander put off his armor and went to his bath, saying, "Let us go and wash off the sweat of battle in the bath of Darius." "No, indeed," said a Companion, "but rather in that of Alexander." And when he saw the basins and pitchers and tubs and caskets, all of gold and curiously wrought, while the apartment was marvelously fragrant with spices and unguents, he turned his eyes upon his Companions and said, "This, as it would seem, is to be a king."

As Alexander was going to supper, someone told him that among the prisoners were the mother, the wife, and two unmarried daughters of Darius whom they believed dead. He sent word to them that Darius was alive and that they need have no fear of Alexander, for it was upon Darius that he was waging war for supremacy; they should have everything that they had thought their due when

Darius was undisputed king. Such are the statements of two historians who were present at the time.

Another report says that on the following day Alexander himself, accompanied only by his bosom friend, Hephaestion, visited Darius' mother. She was in doubt which of them was the king, for they were both dressed in the same way, and went up to Hephaestion, who appeared the taller of the two, prostrating herself before him. When he drew back and one of her attendants pointed out Alexander, saying he was the king, she was ashamed of her mistake and wanted to withdraw. But Alexander told her she had made no mistake, for Hephaestion was also Alexander.

Alexander actually never laid eyes on the wife of Darius, who was reputedly the most beautiful woman in Asia. Years later, though, he married one of her daughters. As for the other captive women, seeing that they were surpassingly stately and beautiful, he merely said jestingly that Persian women were torments to the eyes. According to the Royal Journal, or Diary—the "official" truth and as close to the real truth as we shall ever be able to come—Alexander never had a mistress. Moreover, he drank but rarely, and then it was generally a deliberate action, enabling him to associate freely with comrades from whom his new position was slowly isolating him. His self-restraint and moderation he ascribed to the belief that it was more kingly to conquer himself than others, though his temper always remained his worst enemy. Probably his boastfulness was annoying chiefly to his close associates.

Alexander had come to Asia with a fleet made up of Athenian ships and in part a hostage for Athens' good behavior during his absence. He quickly saw that it was no match for the Phoenician fleet of the Persians, and to avoid the loss of prestige that would follow upon defeat, he disbanded it. After Issus, however, when it might have been advantageous to continue the pursuit of Darius, Alexander realized that he could not leave the Phoenician coast in the hands of the enemy, with their own fleet free to raid Greece. He resolved, therefore, to take the home bases of their fleet and thus bring it over to his side.

It turned out exactly as he expected, though he could not have foreseen the difficulty of taking Tyre, a heavily fortified island half a mile offshore. By building his own fleet as well as a mole to the island, Alexander eventually took Tyre and totally destroyed it. It was a great crime, as great a one as his destruction of rebellious Thebes shortly before his departure from Greece. If, however, a man is to be judged by the standards of morality of his own day, we should add that the destruction of cities was common contemporary practice. Plutarch says that Alexander waged war according to usage and like a king; while Arrian—the second century A.D. historian whose account is the best we have, since it drew from the soundest contemporary sources —remarks that Alexander was the only one of the ancient kings who, from nobility of character, repented the errors he had committed.

Egypt fell to Alexander without a blow, for she hated Persian misrule. On the coast he planned a great city, the first of the seventy-odd cities Alexander founded on his march. His purpose was to give the eastern Mediterranean a commercial and administrative center that might also act, if circumstances warranted, as a link between East and West. Meanwhile, it was essential to provide a commercial substitute for ruined Tyre. The site of Alexandria was chosen with consummate skill, for it was west of the westernmost mouth of the Nile and therefore, thanks to the currents of the Mediterranean, free from the river's silt.

While the army was laying out the city, Alexander and a few friends made a dramatic trip across the Libyan Desert to the oasis of Siwa, to see the oracle of Zeus Ammon, which in Greek eyes was second in importance only to Delphi. It

was a youthful stunt, and Alexander, we must remember, was never anything but young. There was a purpose in it, too, as there generally was with Alexander. He had crossed the Danube a few years earlier to insure his communications. Now he wished to confirm that the desert actually existed and would serve as a natural boundary. Also he could bribe the priests to police the desert for him and, en route, accept the surrender of envoys from Cyrene to the west.

So great was the impression that Alexander made on men's minds that a story soon grew up that Alexander had gone to the oracle to ask about his birth, and that, in fact, he was greeted as the son of Zeus. The story has no foundation in history, and Alexander left Egypt without hearing it. He was intent on finding Darius.

The two kings met for the last time east of the Tigris River at Gaugamela, though the battle popularly takes its name from Arbela, a town nearby. Darius kept his men under arms the entire night before the battle, suspecting a surprise attack, a fact that not only lowered their vitality but added to their natural fear. Alexander, however, followed his usual custom and ordered his soldiers to take dinner and rest themselves. While his Macedonians slept, he himself passed the night in front of his tent with his seer Aristander, celebrating certain mysterious sacred rites and sacrificing to the god Fear. And it is said that the older of his Companions, and particularly Parmenio, when they saw the plain and mountains all lighted up with barbarian fires and heard the sound of voices arising from the enemy camp as if from a vast ocean, were astonished at their multitude and argued that it would be difficult to repel such a tide of war in broad daylight. They therefore came to Alexander's tent after he had finished his sacrifices, and on their behalf Parmenio urged him to make a night attack upon the Persians. But Alexander, realizing the hazards of a battle in the dark, gave them the celebrated reply, "I will not steal my victory."

It was October 1, 331 B.C. The Persian army did not even approach the 1,000,000 infantry and 40,000 cavalry of later legend, but it was larger than the one at Issus—so much larger than Alexander's, indeed, that it extended well beyond his flanks. Alexander's infantry still stood at 30,000 men; the cavalry perhaps had grown to 7,000. As the battle progressed, Darius was again seized with terror and was the first to turn and flee. He hoped to raise a rebellion in eastern Iran, but some months later he was murdered in the Parthian Desert by his cousin, a remarkable prince of Bactria named Bessus. Alexander gave the body a fitting burial.

It is not difficult to imagine Alexander's thoughts as he passed through the lands and capitals of the ancient East, Babylon, Susa, and Persepolis. The hereditary foe of Greece had been utterly defeated, and he was now the ruler of the largest empire the world had ever seen. When he took his seat for the first time under the golden canopy on the royal throne at Persepolis, his old friend, Demaratus of Corinth,

TEXT CONTINUED ON PAGE 47

# A MEDIEVAL VIEW OF ALEXANDER

*Illustrations painted for the Duke of Burgundy*

*Captions from the text of Quintus Curtius Rufus*

Over the centuries after his death, the true story of Alexander's life was enlarged and embroidered until it became the marvelous fabric of fact and fancy known to the Middle Ages as the Romance of Alexander. In the fifteenth century its magic so appealed to the Dukes of Burgundy that they commissioned the finest French artists to illustrate the story in hundreds of miniatures. One of their books was a presentation copy made for Charles the Bold in 1463; the paintings from it, which appear on the following five pages, are here published for the first time.

This book is essentially faithful to history, for it follows the chronicle of Quintus Curtius Rufus, who wrote in Latin in the first century A.D. (The following captions are abridged from his text.) But in these miniatures, familiar figures often assume strange shapes. Fully grown Persian princesses have become dolls sitting in the lap of Queen Mother Sisygambis; 25,000 barbarians throwing rocks on the Greek army in a mountain pass loom as six lone men; and the elephants of King Porus, standing on straight-pegged legs, have trunks that end in nozzles, and ears of Afghan hounds—yet the cumbersome creatures gallop with the speed of race horses.

*"Now they had reached the women; force and lust were not sparing even their persons. But the captive mother and wife of Darius had turned the eyes of all upon themselves. The latter had taken into her arms a young son; but in the lap of their grandmother lay two grown-up maidens, her granddaughters."*

"*Alexander* [in crowned helmet] *sent heralds to urge the Tyrians to make peace; but these they killed and threw into the sea* [right]. *Upon this, the king, greatly angered, resolved to besiege the city. He began to build a causeway which the Tyrians encircled with light craft and assailed with missiles.*"

"*He chose for the city the present site of Alexandria, which derives its name from its founder. Embracing all the ground between the lake and the sea, he planned a circuit of 80 stadia for the walls and left men to take charge of building the city. Seers predicted that many newcomers would dwell there.*"

*"He decided to visit the oracle of Jupiter Ammon. As the king drew near, the eldest of the priests called him son, declaring that his father Jupiter gave him that name. Alexander [kneeling] said that he accepted it, forgetful of his human condition. The prophet declared he would be ruler of all lands."*

*"He with a light armed band entered Persia and the pass which the Persians call the Susidan Gates. Ariobarzanes with 25,000 foot soldiers had taken possession of that pass, from the summit of which they rolled stones of huge size down the slopes and crushed not only single soldiers but entire troops."*

*"Alexander was not far from Persepolis when a wretched troop met the king. They were Greek captives to the number of nearly 4,000 on whom the Persians had inflicted various kinds of torture. The king, having dried his tears, bade them have a good heart, since they would soon see their cities and wives."*

*"Alexander began to consider how he might usurp divine honors. Hermolaus, a high-born Macedonian, and other members of the troop formed a plot to kill the king. They were put to death with torments by those who wished to show their loyalty. Callisthenes also expired in torture although guiltless."*

"*When Alexander had entered the bounds of India, the petty kings of the neighboring race met him intending to submit to him, saying that he was the third son of Jupiter who had arrived in that land. The king received them courteously and bade them follow, intending to use them as guides for his routes.*"

"*Alexander [standing before the tent] came to the river Hydaspes on whose further bank Porus had taken position, intending to prevent the enemy from crossing, with archers with heavier arrows. Light skirmishing took place, for by these small contests both kings were testing the outcome of the main struggle.*"

*"Alexander sent against the elephants the light-armed Agriani and the Thracians. These cast a great shower of weapons upon the elephants and those who were guiding them. Porus, abandoned by his followers, had suffered nine wounds. He urged his elephant to flight [background], pursued by Alexander."*

*"Intending to make for the ocean with a thousand ships, he left Porus and Taxiles, the Indian kings [kneeling] in friendly relations and established each in his own sovereignty. Then he sailed down the river, advancing about 40 stadia each day, to allow the troops to be landed in convenient places."*

TEXT CONTINUED FROM PAGE 40

burst into tears and declared that those Greeks were deprived of great pleasure who had died before seeing Alexander seated on the throne of Darius. Acting against Parmenio's advice, Alexander deliberately set fire to the palace, in order that the world might clearly understand that one regime had given way to another. Legend created from this the fanciful story of Thais, the Athenian courtesan who incited the banqueters to the act and thus punished the Persians for their evil deeds. But the cold fact was that the rule of the Persians had come to an end; so, too, had the war of revenge.

The death of Darius confirmed what the sword had already proclaimed, that Alexander was in fact the Great King of the former Persian Empire. Determined to hold and organize his conquests, he recognized the necessity of examining and possessing his state. He probably considered this a relatively easy task, though the flight of Bessus, Darius' murderer, to Bactria (northern Afghanistan) had its own implications. Bactria was an extensive and solid area of Iranian rule, where the Indo-Europeans preserved much of their early vigor and vitality; still, Alexander had no way of guessing that nationalism in eastern Iran would give him the longest and stiffest resistance in his career.

In the course of the march to Bactria and Sogdiana (Russian Turkestan) there occurred one of the great tragedies of Alexander's life. This was the conspiracy of Philotas. Philotas' family was ancient and proud and had fought nobly for Philip and Alexander. Parmenio, his father, had recently been brushed aside by Alexander and left at Ecbatana; two of his brothers had died during the expedition. Moreover, Alexander's endless marches into an utterly unknown world were preventing the conquerors from settling down to the enjoyment of their gains. Most important of all, perhaps, was the fact that in Macedonia the king was little better than the nobles, and yet here was Alexander grown powerful and aloof, often acting and thinking strangely. Had not the time come, thought Philotas, for the Macedonian nobles to take things into their own hands?

When the plot against Alexander was discovered, Philotas was brought before the army, as Macedonian law required. He confessed and was killed by the soldiers with their javelins. Alexander then sent orders to the generals at Ecbatana to put Parmenio to death also—an action, it has always been said, that marks the darkest moment in his life; in later eyes, it was plain murder. Yet an ancient Macedonian law decreed that relatives of a conspirator against the king must also die. The execution of Parmenio was judicial, although it is difficult to believe that Alexander, had he wished, could not have persuaded the army to a different action in the case of a man to whom he owed so much. Probably he decided to let the famous general pay the penalty of the law in order to break the Macedonian opposition to him.

Alexander had indeed been displaying dramatically strange ideas and actions ever since he first set foot in Asia. It is quite impossible, at this point in his career, to put a label on them and say what he had in mind, but the end result was one of the greatest revolutions in the history of thought. Alexander had acquired, it should be remembered, the Greek point of view toward barbarians (non-Greeks). Plato had held that all barbarians were enemies of the Greeks by nature; and Aristotle, as we have already remarked, said that all barbarians were slaves by nature, especially those of Asia. Now let us observe Alexander's extraordinary capacity for rapid growth along many lines.

Alexander had come to Asia Minor in a dual capacity, as king of Macedon and commander in chief of the League of Corinth. Soon he became the ally of the Greek cities along the Asia Minor coast, the adopted son of a native queen, Ada of Caria, and the Great King at least in the interior districts. This latter title became his in actual fact not much later, and before his death he was also the suzerain of Indian rajahs, and a god in both Greece and Egypt. In working out his position in the state, his solution was to take over the existing forms of government and to assume a different relation to the various sections of the empire, much in the manner of the British monarch of a later day. More extraordinary than his allowing the queen of a barbarian people to adopt him—to show that he had come as *their* king, too—was his appointment of two barbarians as governors of provinces in Asia Minor. Then, he asserted his independence of the Corinthian league by not punishing Darius' captured Greek mercenaries, but adding them to his own army. Finally, he began a significant improvement on the Persian administrative system by separating the military, civil, and financial powers of the provincial governors. All this he did in eighteen months, during which

TEXT CONTINUED ON PAGE 50

FROM *The Generalship of Alexander the Great* BY J. F. C. FULLER; EYRE & SPOTTISWOODE, LONDON, 1958

*T*he last encounter between Alexander and Darius occurred at Gaugamela and continued the next day on the plains of Arbela, seen stretching out beyond the mound of Keramlais, east of the Tigris in Iraq. The site was especially chosen by the Persian king since the flat land would facilitate the swift attacks of his charging cavalry.

47

"This day," said Darius, "will establish or end the greatest empire any age has seen." The battle fought that day — October 1, 331 B.C. — on the plain of Arbela has been depicted by Albrecht Altdorfer in a painting which, for intricacy of detail, is without parallel in the history of art. Out of his imagination the sixteenth-century German artist created a vast landscape of plain, mountain, sea and sky, castles and cities, the Persian camp and the battling armies. The Greeks, surging across the scene from the right, have just broken the Persian line. Darius, in a chariot drawn by three white horses, races for the mountain refuge, pursued by Alexander in golden armor, with poised lance. Symbolic darkness closes over the Persian horde while the rays of the sun fall upon the victorious army of the West, and a legend in the sky proclaims: "Alexander the Great finally defeats Darius after having killed about 100,000 foot soldiers and 10,000 horsemen, and having captured Darius' mother, wife and children, who were fleeing in disorder with 10,000 horsemen."

TEXT CONTINUED FROM PAGE 47

time he had also won two pitched battles with the Persians and overcome various strong cities and mountain tribes.

The conclusion of the war of revenge, which the burning of the palace at Persepolis helped to signalize, meant also the end of Alexander's reliance on his Greek allies. Not much later, therefore, he dismissed them all and allowed those who wished (as most of them did) to re-enlist in his imperial army. Was this an indication of a rapidly growing personal dominion, or was it his way of showing the vast barbarian world that the Greeks were not to occupy a privileged position, that all peoples were to be treated equally? A clue may be found in Alexander's adoption of Persian dress for occasional wear at this time, though once again we have the hostile gossip to the effect that Alexander was giving himself up more and more to Oriental luxury and indeed, that he had a retinue of concubines.

The actual question that Alexander was confronting was simply whether he was to substitute Greek despotism for Oriental—that is, whether it was to be the same old world, or whether a new state could be formed along very different lines. We learn from Plutarch that Alexander considered it his kingly business to mix all men as in a loving cup. Alexander had been able to test Greek smugness by contact with barbarians, on the battlefield and off, and experience had convinced him of the essential sameness of all people. It was in Egypt, Plutarch continues, that Alexander accepted the teaching of the philosopher Psammon, that all mankind is under the kingship of God. Still more philosophical, Plutarch adds, was Alexander's own opinion that although God is indeed a common father of all mankind, still, He makes peculiarly His own the noblest and best of men.

To give concrete expression to these ideas, to create a common bond within his world state, was Alexander's hardest task. For the moment, at least, his founding of cities had to suffice. Usually these were not wholly new cities, as is generally supposed, but rather existing settlements to which he added old or wounded soldiers. They were located at strategic points and were intended to police the countryside and guard communications. But, of course, the soldiers were Greeks and Macedonians (the distinction between the

ARAB INFORMATION CENTER

*"Alexander's Entry Into Babylon"*

*Babylon Today*

*I*n triumph Alexander entered Babylon, a winter capital of the Persian kings, barely three years after he had crossed into Asia. Quintus Curtius describes the scene: "A great part of the Babylonians had taken their places on the walls . . . Bagophanes, guardian of the citadel and of the royal funds, had strewn the whole road with flowers and garlands and had placed here and there on both sides silver altars which he had piled high, not only with frankincense but with perfumes of all kinds." At dusk the citizens spread the streets with the "naptha" which oozed from their oil-rich land, then set it afire to light the sky and amaze the conqueror.

This splendid scene was painted by Charles Lebrun for the splendor-loving king of France, Louis XIV. The court of Versailles might have pondered in it the transitory nature of earthly glory. For after Alexander left Babylon for eight years of hard campaigning, he returned to it only in time to die. And Babylon itself, in succeeding centuries, vanished beneath the surface of the earth. At left is all that remains today of what Plutarch called "this richest of cities."

51

two peoples was soon forgotten) and from these islands of Hellenism, or Greek culture, there spread a knowledge of Greek ways which, as Alexander hoped, helped to unite the peoples of his empire. The Hellenization of Hither Asia, as it turned out, was the most important specific result of Alexander's life.

These, then, were the chief "strange" ideas that Alexander had held up to the time of Parmenio's execution. It is little wonder that he should exclaim that Hephaestion was the only friend to understand and approve his plans of empire.

In the spring of 329 B.C. Alexander crossed the Hindu Kush into Bactria by the Khawak Pass. Almost at once his most important body of Greek cavalry, which had been under the executed Parmenio, rebelled and was sent home. The resentment of these men at the death of their beloved commander and their subsequent dismissal presented Alexander with the greatest crisis in his life. Should he himself also return? Obviously he could not find more Greeks and Macedonians at a moment's notice, and yet his entire expedition might end in disaster at this point. There was only one thing to do: to take a chance and, for the first time, to incorporate large numbers of Asiatics in his army.

Alexander's willingness to trust his own personal safety and the success of his expedition to barbarians must be placed at the top of the extraordinary ideas that now rapidly took form and unfolded to the world. And their motivation was the immediate need for survival.

The new Asiatic troops proved invaluable to Alexander during the two years in Bactria-Sogdiana. It was a time of guerrilla warfare, of constant marching, ambushes and treachery, of wounds and sickness. The opposition of the Macedonian nobility, moreover, remained; and one night at a banquet Alexander was taunted about his great debt to Philip and Philip's men. Finally, thoroughly drunk as he was this evening, he let his terrible temper get the better of him, and he murdered Clitus "the Black," as he was called, a friend since boyhood who had saved the King's life at the Granicus.

Somehow or other during these same two years, as we have said, Alexander found time to think. If the Asiatic troops were so loyal, could not some gesture be made to placate eastern Iran and bring the guerrilla warfare to an end? His solution was to marry Roxane, the captive daughter of a Bactrian prince, whom the soldiers pronounced the most beautiful of all the women they had seen in Asia,

with the single exception of Darius' wife. Legend turned it into a love affair, but it was a political marriage, the beginning of a real effort to take Asia into full partnership with him. This, and the desire to legitimize his rule, led him in the year before his death also to marry Barsine, Darius' daughter. At that time, most of his friends took barbarian wives, and gifts were distributed to those soldiers, 10,000 in number, who in the course of all the marching had taken up more or less permanently with Asiatic girls.

Alexander's idea of a fusion of races did not mean that he planned a deliberate Hellenization of the East or a barbarization of the Greeks and Macedonians. Those who wished were free to pursue their own national life—and they represented the overwhelming majority—but at the same time there was to develop a new life based on an interchange and mixture of customs and blood. This new attitude toward the world was to be the driving and unifying force of his empire. As part of this program, he now ordered that 30,000 native youths should be taught the Greek language and trained in the use of Macedonian weapons. And to leave no doubt that these ideas were to be applied on an immense scale, he revealed his intention, once he had finished with the East, of marching against the

*On the hot, dry plain of eastern Persia the ruins of Persepolis still stand against the sky as they have stood for more than two thousand years since Alexander put this conquered city to the torch. Beyond the columns of the Apadana, or audience hall, may be seen the remnants of the royal palace, built by the early Achaemenid kings, Darius I and his son Xerxes I, predecessors of Darius III whom Alexander defeated. Here the Persian monarchs exercised their double powers as temporal kings and as earthly vicars of the great divinity Ahura Mazda. It was to break this double power, some historians theorize, that Alexander, acting for himself and Zeus, ordered the city burned. "Such," we are told, "was the end of the capital of the entire Orient from which so many nations previously sought jurisdiction, the birthplace of so many kings, once the special terror of Greece . . . And not even in the long age that followed its destruction did it rise again."*

West, to Italy and beyond. This was one of the first manifestations, surely, of a growing megalomania.

But what to do about an uncertain officer corps, as represented by the Macedonian opposition? Here was an immediate military problem, deserving treatment as drastic as that meted out to the mutiny of his cavalry. Alexander reached the decision to abandon the comradely relationship with his officers that had long characterized the Macedonian monarchy, and to put an end to wavering support and possible plots by becoming an autocrat. Or better, to put it in Greek terms, he decided, in this century which had already raised living men to divine status, to become a god.

The plan fell through for the moment, but when we look at Alexander's extraordinary ideas—on world conquest and his own relation to the state, on the use of barbarians in administration and army, the foundation of cities, a common culture, personal deification—we must conclude that there was no way to realize them except by autocratic action. Ideas, however, have a way of growing. In the year before his death, during a banquet of reconciliation with his men after another brief mutiny, Alexander prayed for partnership in the empire and for unity and concord in a joint commonwealth where all peoples were to be partners rather than subjects. It was this prayer, it has been said, that marks a revolution in human thought. It was picked up, first by Zeno, whose Stoicism preached the brotherhood of man, and then by Saint Paul in his stirring vision of a world in which there shall be "neither Greek nor Jew, barbarian nor Scythian, bond nor free."

When the time came to leave eastern Iran, Alexander

*This highly romantic version of* The Marriage of Roxane and Alexander *by the Renaissance artist Il Sodoma, bears little relation to the fact that this was a political union intended to end the guerrilla resistance of the eastern Iranian tribesmen. The painting is based on a description given by Lucian, a rhetorician of the second century A.D., of a painting on the same theme done by the Greek painter Aëtion, a contemporary of Alexander. Of the original painting, Lucian wrote: "A splendid bridal bed is seen on which Roxane, in the sweet flower of her youth, shy and coy sits, in front of Alexander standing. Smiling cupids hover around her. One pulls off one of her stockings; one removes her veil from behind as if to show her to her spouse. Another kindly unlaces her sandal, whilst yet another, laughing, is pulling Alexander towards her by a flap of his coat. The king is seen offering a crown to the maid." In Il Sodoma's painting, Roxane's attendants have just finished the ceremonial ablutions and prepare to withdraw. On the right bearing a torch, Alexander's friend and best man, Hephaestion, stands with Hymen, the god of marriage, gazing wistfully at the royal couple.*

recrossed the Hindu Kush by the Kaoshan Pass and continued down the Khyber Pass to India. This ancient land, with its ascetics and Brahmans, its marvels and curious customs, filled the Greeks with awe. But Alexander hurried on, for, being wholly ignorant of the size of India and even of the existence of China, he thought that Ocean—the great sea, so men believed, that ringed the inhabited land—lay not much farther east. A few years earlier, standing beside the Caspian Sea, he believed it to be a northern gulf of Ocean and organized an exploring expedition to find out. Now he thought he was near the eastern and natural limit of his empire, where great cities and harbors of his creation would produce a wonderful prosperity and serve to tie together in an economic whole the various sections of the state.

As Alexander traversed the Punjab, however, the great Indian rajah Porus opposed his crossing of the Hydaspes River, now known as the Jhelum. Alexander won a victory over him at great cost; but when, not much later, his men stood upon the high bank of the Hyphasis and gazed across the interminable plains extending to the horizon, their spirits sank. The rumor of more enemies, of men larger and braver than the other Indians, and of countless elephants, unsettled a morale that had already been weakened by the recent fighting. During the past eight and a half years Alexander's men had marched over 11,000 miles. Fatigued mentally and physically, they could not see the purpose of further marching and fighting in unknown lands. When Alexander learned that the army would go no farther and insisted upon returning home, he retired to his tent for three days—like Achilles—and hoped that the men would change their minds. But it was of no avail.

It had been a curious mutiny, for it had never occurred to the army to depose Alexander, the only man who could bring them safely home. To mark the farthest point of his advance Alexander erected twelve tremendous altars to the Olympian gods and offered sacrifice upon them, and celebrated gymnastic and cavalry contests. He also prepared armor that was larger than usual, and stalls for horses that were higher and bits that were heavier than those in common use, and left them scattered up and down to impress later generations with the manner of men who had come that way.

Alexander's men won their point, but it was he who chose the route home. In November, 326 B.C., the army, aboard ship and on foot, began the descent of the Indus river system. Indescribable slaughter followed their progress, but in July of the following year the Indian Ocean was reached. Alexander's joy at seeing the southern limit of the inhabited world was great. All that now remained was to explore the route by land and sea between the Indus and Mesopotamia, and the empire would be a well-knit and self-sufficient whole.

Alexander knew something of the difficulties that lay ahead, for he had already sent westward, by a different route, many of his troops, most of his baggage, and his elephants. (He was too good a general to use the beasts in battle, for he recognized their unreliability, but he did employ them for transport and in hunting.) He had no real conception, however, of the torrid, arid wastes awaiting him, especially the 150 terrible desert miles in Baluchistan. His journey became one of the greatest marches in military history. His commissariat, for the only time in the expedition, failed him, and he was unable to keep in touch with the fleet under Nearchus. Most of the camp followers died, but he got his army of 15,000 men back safely to Persepolis early in 324 B.C., almost exactly six years after his first triumphant entry.

Plans of further conquest, of the administration of his empire, of the exploration of Arabia, now filled Alexander's mind. But it was too much for him. His ceaseless mental and physical activity, the immense responsibilities of state, his long marches and dangerous wounds had so lowered his vitality that he was unable to throw off a fever. On June 13, 323 B.C., Alexander died at Babylon, not yet thirty-three years of age, after a reign of twelve years and eight months.

The world was never again to be the same. Gone forever, at least as a force in politics, was the small democratic city-state of the Greeks; gone, too, was the homogeneous civilization concentrated around the Aegean Sea. The high standards of taste, the freedom, responsibility, and intensity of Periclean life became things of the past. The world now belonged to the large monarchic state.

Nothing could be further from the truth than to imagine that, because Alexander's empire upon his death broke up

APOLLO

56

BUDDHA

# FROM APOLLO TO BUDDHA

*O*ne strange and lasting result of Alexander's march to the East was the image of Buddha. Before the Greeks arrived in Asia, Buddha was never represented in painting or sculpture. His horse might be shown—riderless—or his throne—vacant—but no Oriental artist ventured to carve or draw his sacred person. The Greeks who followed Alexander into India took with them statues of their gods, which became the inspiration of sculptors in the northern frontier province of Gandhara. There in the second century A.D. appear the first images of Buddha, clearly modeled on Apollo. The native sculptors kept the Greek profile and topknot but gave Buddha a more contemplative expression and added the Oriental feature of a third "eye" in the forehead. Gradually, over the centuries, the image spread eastward and was metamorphosed into a purely Oriental figure, in both features and dress. As shown below, the Gandhara sculptors modeled the Buddha's dress on the Greek toga but made it soft and clinging, as if changing the fabric from Greek wool to Indian silk; later the lines of the toga disappear altogether. But the Apollonian topknot remains to this day to mark the Western origin of the Buddha image.

SOCRATES IN GREEK TOGA

GANDHARA SCULPTURE

LATER CHINESE BUDDHA

57

into three or four large states, his conquests came to naught. The new kingdoms that resulted were ruled by Macedonians and Greeks for three centuries along Western lines, until the coming of Rome. The most striking fact about the Hellenistic age—as we term those extraordinary centuries after Alexander's death, when Hellenism was adopted by non-Greeks—is the unity of the large world that had been opened by his expedition.

Macedonians and Greeks who had been left behind in Bactria eventually mustered enough strength to march again across the Hindu Kush and conquer India as far as Calcutta. In the region of the Khyber Pass known as Gandhara, they created an art that was an extraordinary mixture of East and West. Hitherto Buddha had been merely an abstraction in art, but the only way Greek sculptors knew how to represent a god was in the form of a man. Thus when Chinese pilgrims to Buddha's birthplace passed through Gandhara, they brought back with them the new conception of Buddha. Except for this, however, the Farther East would be exactly the same today had Alexander and his men never existed.

It was distinctly otherwise westward. If some of Alexander's dreams took root slowly, such as that of co-operation between peoples, nevertheless his idea of the *oikoumenē*, the "inhabited world," found immediate acceptance. In the

---

### Alexander in his own defense

*In answer to Hermolaus, whom he later put to death for conspiring against his life, Alexander said:*

He says, the Persians, whom we have conquered, are in high honour with me! In my opinion at least, the surest indication of my moderation is that I do not rule even the vanquished tyrannically. For I came into Asia, not in order to overthrow nations and make a desert of a half part of the world, but in order that those whom I had subdued in war might not regret my victory. . . .

That possession is not lasting of which we are made owners by the sword; the gratitude for acts of kindness is everlasting. If we wish to hold Asia, not merely to pass through it, our clemency must be shared with its people, their faith in us will make a stable and lasting empire. . . .

I see in many nations things which we should not blush to imitate; and so great an empire cannot fitly be ruled without contributing some things to the vanquished and learning from them. . . . Would that the people of India may believe me to be a god. For wars depend upon reputation, and often even what has been falsely believed has gained the place of truth.

Do you think it was to gratify my luxury that I adorned your arms with gold and silver? I wished to show to those who are accustomed to nothing cheaper than those metals that the Macedonians, who are invincible in other things, cannot be outdone even in gold. It is this glory, parricide that you are, that you wished to interrupt and to deliver the Macedonians to the conquered nations by killing their king!

---

Hellenistic age man thought of himself more and more as a member of a world society, a society in which there might be (and were) sharp differences, but in which a common culture nevertheless acted as a natural bond. The new culture was different from that of Periclean days, for it was affected by the rapid rise of the ordinary man and by close contact with Orientalism. There could be no more vivid illustration of the unity of the world than the fact that the New Testament was written in Greek.

It was the culture of the Hellenistic age that civilized Rome and facilitated her creation of her own world state and then Christianity's conquest of that state. Only a mighty historical force could have brought that state into being. As such it is Alexander's monument; while his dreams have been, and still are, a challenge to humanity to substitute the idea of universalism, of solidarity of the world and co-operation between peoples, for narrowness of race and outlook.

*C. A. Robinson, Jr., Professor of Classics at Brown University, is one of the world's leading experts on Alexander. His latest book,* The History of Alexander the Great, *is a study of surviving historical material on Alexander's life. His other works on Alexander include* The Ephemerides of Alexander's Expedition *and a popular narrative biography,* Alexander the Great.

---

"When they asked to whom he left his kingdom, he replied, to him who was the best man, and when asked when he wished divine honors to be paid to him, he said that he wished it at the time when they themselves were happy. These were the king's last words and shortly afterwards he died." (Quintus Curtius.) This seventeenth-century Persian miniature of the dying Alexander testifies to the grief that prevailed in the Orient. The Persians called him a most just and mild lord and vowed that no other had been more worthy to rule them. Even the Macedonians confessed their ingratitude in having withheld the divine honors which Alexander coveted in his lifetime.

*Williams in Rutherford, New Jersey*

# William Carlos Williams, M.D.

*By* PAUL ENGLE

*Homage from one poet to another is an old and handsome tradition in letters. Here a younger poet from America's middle western prairies pays tribute in his own way to one of America's most admired elder creative spirits—a lifelong resident of industrial New Jersey and a veteran practitioner of medicine there besides. A full generation and half a continent separate Paul Engle, author of* American Child, *of many other books of poetry and prose, and teacher at the State University of his native Iowa, from Dr. William Carlos Williams of Rutherford, New Jersey, at seventy-five the holder of many poetry prizes and awards and a lasting figure in anthologies. Yet a common dedication across the broad lands of the Republic links them both.*

Bill Williams lives back east in Rutherford, New Jersey
(called in the black of time by the Indians, Boiling Springs,
but the springs are buried now or turned into sewers).
He lives near the civil and hill-rising Passaic River.

I live out in Iowa where the corn leaves shake all summer
beyond the bull-shouldered Mississippi River,
but a lot of people out here know about Dr. W. C. Williams.
He has delivered more babies than any other poet in history—
two thousand, to be exact—dragged into the world
as live and kicking as his own poems. Between mending
bones and bellies and even that soft-tough organ the brain,
he has worked at mending the language.

Read his poems out loud and hear,
beyond and through the broken lines,
the motion of a man's voice speaking.
The live words jump and quiver in the common air.

Bill Williams is a man devoted to the human race,
loving its power for love and meanness, clearly
knowing it has the grace to pick your pocket
when you bend down to help as it lies injured,
kicking and screaming there on the stone street.
He didn't get that way by reading books the professors
chop out of each other's knowledge like salt blocks.
He learned by diving into the dark pool of life
as a boy into the pool under the Passaic Falls.
He accepted the whole dirt and delight of it.
The lure of libraries, calling men to their safe
and feminine caves, has never gentled him.

Like a man wading a rapid river, to keep his footing
he keeps moving.

He has walked the streets of a named city,
feeling the concrete hard under his leather shoe.
Liking the people there, he has not lamented
the quick deer driven back to the Ramapo hills.
In the fret and fume of that place he has done his job
with deft hands, refreshed by his work as other men by play,
a damn good doctor
for all kinds of men and women and their snot-nosed kids.

He does not mourn wildflowers bulldozed into the ditch
for homes with families he visited with his medicines
compounded from gentian, ginseng and digitalis.

He has taken the real world of virus and grass,
of microscope and factory, of the corner wind
blowing dust in his eyes, and made a true vision
of reality out of it. From artless things that
simply stand up hard in the ravaging daylight

in all of their blunt thingness, he has made
a hard and honest art.

He has listened to many voices on American streets,
in stores and hospitals, talking about weather, war,
pains, politics, gossip, and heard that speech
go up and down with a new twist to the old words.

It wasn't English porridge he wanted for breakfast,
but Quaker Oats, made in Cedar Rapids, Iowa,
with a picture of Ben Franklin big on the box,
from grain raised in the long middlewestern bread basket
that runs a thousand miles from the old Appalachians
to the young, rough Rockies.

Like the antibiotics he learned to use, his poems
heal and are healthy.

He is still good for a laugh, driving his wit
like a new nail between anxiety and despair.

He still wants to know men and women so closely
he can look into the whites of their eyes and catch
the flicker of health or illness there, and find
their individual smells with his curious nose.

No vagueness for him as doctor—the disease
hunted, named, fought.

No vagueness for him as poet—always the bright
particulars, as a doctor works with the definite
fever, bone, fear. No universals for him apart
from the precise thing—not the general color of red,
but that exact geranium in its tin can, rusted and red.

He lays his hands on the body of this world,
punching the pain,
finding the cold dread and the warm desire,
the hungry tissue and the voluptuous gland,
the mixed-up rapture, reek and wonder of it.

He writes what he sees, the poet of what is there.
Nothing to be concealed, neither the dark blood
of the internally bleeding gut, nor the white
shadow of love a man and a woman cast in the hidden night.

He has an animal's memory of places, Cholla
seen from a passing train, Paris walked in slowly,
remembering how he went as a boy through all that
shaped stone and the shapeless crowds,
the hills of west Jersey glowing in their greenness,
the halls of the old French hospital in New York
torn down for the Lincoln Tunnel.

A man of this world, knowing its human hate,
the wildness padding through our mind's civilized jungle,
but still believing in men, women and children,
still trusting their betrayed idealisms, fond of their affections,
hopeful of their hopes.

Like any of us who has lived long in one town,
he enjoys driving his car on the familiar streets
where he recognizes the big elms and the little dogs,
the wooden houses where he has felt
the forehead flame and the hand go cold, and heard
the child's voice strangle in the filled-up throat.
He waves to the cops on their way to arrest a speeding truck.
He is a man at home in his own home town.

Now he wants to live in a little house
in his own backyard, close to the mess and marvel
of daily, ordinary, dirty life,
where he does not have to write his poems between patients.

There, like a man shaving the same scraped face,
pulling his cheek sideways, he can let the steam of his poems
rise from the warm bowl of his imagination.

There he can delight in the eye colored with looking,
the ear beaten and blessed with the machine roar of our time,
with the lively, pleading, bitter, lovely words
yelled down the streets of his town, the kids
calling each other to come on out for one more day
in the loud, clear sun, to throw, to catch, crying,
Come on, Harry, run with it.

His poems rise in the falling flow of our days,
where the hours splatter and float like foam,
as bass once jumped in the pool under the Passaic Falls,
shining and alive. So they will leap and fall
in their lithe quickness, as the years stream over,
around and under them, as long as men use English
words in the steady talk of an American voice.

*Engle in Iowa*

By DWIGHT E. ROBINSON

# THE RULES OF FASHION CYCLES

ILLUSTRATED FOR HORIZON BY DOUGLAS GORSLINE

*Hoop skirts, hobble skirts,*

*gingerbread villas, glass houses—*

*all are instances of*

*ruling styles that end in excess*

*and lead to their opposites.*

*So argues a student of design,*

*presenting his theory of*

*the puzzling behavior of taste.*

The history of succeeding styles observes a few unalterable rules which, even if they do not always appear to be firmly grasped by vice presidents in charge of styling or by consumer researchers, are applicable to all industries. Whether the problem is selling cars, architectural plans, pedigreed dogs, or dresses, the motives which prod consumers into continual revision of their tastes are essentially the same from commodity to commodity.

Despite all the current studies of consumer motivation, however, American management so far has generally failed to grasp the significance of the basic rules of style, or to realize the benefits to be obtained by applying them. Not enough attention has been paid to the underlying secrets of the women's apparel trade, the purest and oldest form of fashion expression, or to the possibilities of studying fashion as an independent behavioral phenomenon rather than as an adjunct to another specialized area of study such as consumer psychology, economic demand, or industrial design.

Part of the explanation of these oversights may lie in a certain provincialism on the part of market researchers, including social scientists. While they have displayed a pronounced and growing tendency to advise product planners, designers, advertisers, and marketing executives in general, all too frequently the researchers have based their advice mainly on inferences drawn from the raw data ob-

*Left: The eighteenth-century taste for extravagant ornamentation reached its height in rococo gowns, towering headdresses, and such florid buildings as this pavilion of the Zwinger Palace in Dresden.*

tained by questionnaires and by interviews, with little knowledge of the social dynamics of taste to guide them. Whether out of masculine disdain or befuddlement in the face of a subject that smacks of womanly vanity, only a few sociologists and psychologists have joined a much larger number of men of letters, museum curators, and the like in exploring the basic theory of fashion.

The behavioral complex underlying all stylistic innovation—by this I mean all changes in design which are not purely the results of engineering advances—can conveniently be summed up under the single word *fashion*. And fashion, defined in its most general sense, is the pursuit of novelty for its own sake. Every market into which the consumer's fashion sense has insinuated itself is, by that very token, subject to this common, compelling need for unceasing change in the styling of its goods.

The reason for this is that the stimuli of fashion derive solely from the *comparisons* that consumers draw between new designs and the old designs they replace. No single style of design, no matter how brilliantly it is conceived, can claim any independent fashion significance at all, nor can it possess more than a fugitive lease on life.

Paul Poiret, the top Paris *couturier* of the 1920's, once summed up his credo by declaring, "All fashions end in excess"—a principle which is the beginning of wisdom for all who are concerned with style policy. He was aware that the overriding responsibility of the designer in a fashion market is the unending provision of novelty. Implicitly he recognized that one of the most exacting problems the stylist ever faces is that of deciding what to do when he has exhausted the possibilities of a current direction in styling emphasis. What does he do, for example, when the waistline, hemline, or any other line has been carried as far as it will go? It is here that the *couturier* must exercise to the utmost every ounce of his insight into the meaning of fashion.

As a *couturier* Poiret knew that the appetite for novelty, arising from the twofold insistence of the lady of fashion on preserving her inimitability from the onslaught of the vulgar and on demonstrating her affluence through unrelenting expenditure on newly cut costumes, is never satisfied with any one mode of presenting the figure. Fashions in dress design subsist on measures to transform or to distort, whether through exaggeration or minimization, the shape and features of the human figure. To illustrate:

¶ The hoop skirts of the eighteenth century and the crinoline of the nineteenth ballooned to diameters of eight feet. As the hip line was exaggerated beyond the point of simply imperiling navigation to the point of making it literally impossible, the waistline was tightened to the point of suffocation and interference with digestion.

¶ In the interim, in the Directoire and Empire periods around 1800, a contrary tendency toward undress was exploited. *La Parisienne's* test of the suitability of a pseudo-

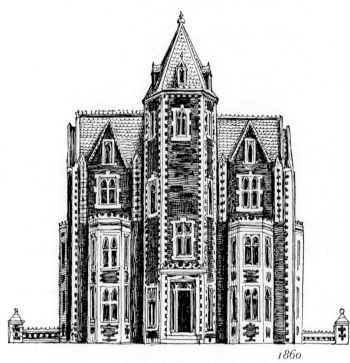

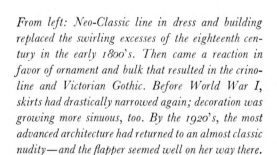

1820

1860

*From left: Neo-Classic line in dress and building replaced the swirling excesses of the eighteenth century in the early 1800's. Then came a reaction in favor of ornament and bulk that resulted in the crinoline and Victorian Gothic. Before World War I, skirts had drastically narrowed again; decoration was growing more sinuous, too. By the 1920's, the most advanced architecture had returned to an almost classic nudity—and the flapper seemed well on her way there.*

classical gown of transparent silk was to see whether she could easily draw it through a ring taken from her little finger. The last resort of modesty was flesh-colored tights.

¶ The flapper of the Jazz Age, though she was in her turn the despair of her late-Victorian parents, never dashed about in quite the dishabille of Mme Récamier, but what she missed in transparency she made up for with leg display.

Whether at a given time the particular form of emphasis is toward padding out or constricting, toward concealment or exposure, once such a movement is launched it must be intensified each season, ensuring that the ultrafashionable will be able to disport themselves in more of a good thing than their less favored contemporaries.

*1910*

*1925*

The most important corollary of Poiret's axiom is this: a fashion can never retreat gradually and in good order. Like a dictator it must always expand its aggressions—or collapse. Old fashions never just fade away; they die suddenly and arbitrarily.

The reason for this is simple and logically inescapable. The one thing fashion cannot stand is to repeat the recently outmoded style, the passé. Better for the lady of fashion to look like a freak than to be mistaken for her grocer's wife dolled up in a cheap version of something she herself sported a year or two ago. For instance:

¶ The hoop skirts of the French court and the crinoline of a century later did not gradually contract: they both exploded in a fragmentation of trains, loops, and bustles.

¶ Within a decade after court ladies found it necessary to crouch on the floor of their coaches so as to accommodate their soaring headdresses, Lady Hamilton (Nelson's Emma) was enthralling the court of Naples and eminent visitors such as Goethe with her "classical attitudes," for which her main props were no more than her own silky curls, a few yards of gauze, and a pet dove or two. And it was not long before thousands of less notorious ladies were taking her cue.

¶ Again, a couple of generations later, after such devices as the bustle and the leg-of-mutton sleeve exhausted the expansionist tendencies of late-Victorian days, the shirtwaist and hobble skirt were suddenly introduced, clearing the way for the boyish skimpiness of the 1920's.

65

As we shall see later in greater detail, the rule that fashion never smoothly retraces its footsteps demonstrates itself even in the history of architecture, which is a particularly stern testing ground.

Look at what happened to the arch when, at the end of the late Gothic style, it had reached the extreme of pointedness. Did the Tudor architects, seeing that matters had reached a geometric impasse, decide to blunt it just a bit? Not at all. With unerring wisdom they squashed it almost flat, making it a perfect frame for Henry VIII. The royal tailors had, meanwhile, taken care to pad his already thick physique to something closely approaching a true square.

What lies behind these swift and extreme changes? If functional criteria could be more precisely defined, the game of fashion change might be interpreted as a series of departures from, and returns to, the norm of function. Unfortunately, this is not the case. Function is permissive. Even nature's experiments in animals—on land, in the sea, in the air—reveal that the laws of locomotion or mechanics permit a kaleidoscopic variety of anatomical forms.

The designer has learned that the usefulness of a garment, together with all the functional criteria surrounding utility, is a consideration of only incidental relevance to his purposes. Naturally, he is more than willing to play up the merits of a new design by claiming that it permits greater freedom of movement, better accentuates the feminine figure, or is more suitable to modern living. But he does this with tongue in cheek. He is only too aware that, judging by results, the aims of feminine coquetry have been as well served by the dress designs of one era as by those of another.

The safest thing that can be said of costume variation is that it veers between extremes of overdressing and underdressing, although there are many other variables. Perusal of the fashion journals suggests that when one of these extremes has been reached, the recourse that has typically proved most successful is swift return to a form of compromise, or golden mean, which lies about halfway between overdress and underdress. Such norms are loosely referred to as "classical" styles in the dress trade. In turn, they serve as points of departure toward an alternative extreme.

The *couturier* is then likely to visit the art galleries or museums to seek inspiration from the designs of past eras. (At the Metropolitan Museum of Art in New York, for instance, the women's apparel industry maintains a Costume Institute, where thousands of dresses going back several centuries are carefully preserved, catalogued, and made available for inspection by qualified visitors from the garment district.) He will also, of course, give careful heed to technological advances in the form of new materials or new mechanical dressmaking aids, as well as to arising needs of contemporary living, in shaping his patterns to present-day conditions. As Christian Dior put it, "There is room for audacity in the framework of tradition." It is an arresting thought that relics of the past, together with fruits of indus-

trial progress, so frequently form the chief supports of the game of novelty that is fashion.

In sharp contrast to the volatility of fashion styling, the problems the designer faces in devising a product that is functionally serviceable are comparatively stable; at the most he needs to make adjustments for technological advances. But even in industries where engineering advances are especially rapid, they do not make themselves felt in the same remorseless way, season after season, as in the case of fashion demand.

Furthermore, function is obviously the sole basis for distinguishing one commodity from another. Fashion, on the other hand, is concerned only with appearances, with decoration. While decoration must always to some extent adapt itself to the function of the article it embellishes, it is still very much an end in itself. It is in this respect that the problems involved in styling changes are essentially the same from industry to industry.

A look at the home and its decoration will illustrate my thesis. In thus shifting our attention from dresses to buildings, we make a long leap from one of the most ephemeral forms of decoration to one of the most enduring. From this vantage point we can see the more stable, long-range forces operating on the mainstream of stylistic development. For the obvious reasons that houses are extremely durable and are major items of expenditure, a family's taste must necessarily be frozen for a long time, if not for a lifetime.

As far as the study of style changes is concerned, however, the differences between architectural trends and fashion trends should not be overestimated. Surprising as it may seem, the long-term, society-wide swings between the two extreme poles of elaboration and ornamentation, on the one hand, and simplicity and functionalism, on the other, dominate the exterior and interior decoration of the home just as powerfully and unfailingly as they do costume. Despite the pronounced differences in durability between the two media, the timing of these swings in each case is almost exactly parallel. For example:

¶ When the Neo-Classical style succeeded the Rococo toward the end of the eighteenth century, "noble simplicity" was as much the ideal in the fine arts, including architecture, as comparative undress was the fancy of the lady of fashion.

¶ The crinoline corresponded with the overloaded gingerbread façade in the heyday of Victorianism.

¶ The flapper of the 1920's witnessed the onslaught of the stripped-down, modernistic edifice.

True, fashions in dress, which can be discarded so readily, do exhibit a much greater frequency of short-term excursions and alarms, but there the difference ends.

Perhaps this over-all parallelism is not so surprising after all. As psychologists have pointed out, the symbolism inherent in the house and its furnishings is only one degree less intimate and personal than that of dress itself. It is hard

CONTINUED ON PAGE 113

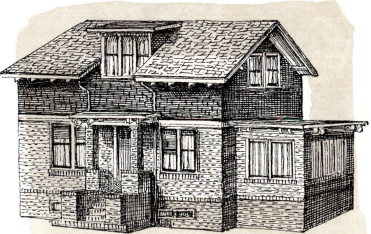

ERA OF COOLIDGE

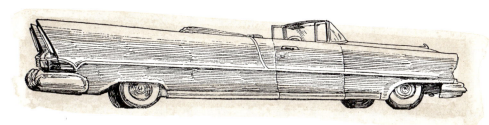

ERA OF EISENHOWER
(MIDDLE)

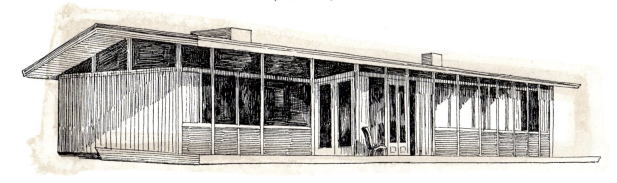

ERA OF EISENHOWER
(LATE)

*Automobile silhouettes have generally corresponded to prevailing taste in domestic architecture. The gaunt, boxy shapes of the twenties (top) gave way to the long, low look of today (middle). But the new popularity of foreign cars and "split-levels" (bottom) suggests a return to height and angularity.*

# The Debut of the
# Picture Interview

On the eve of his one hundred and first birthday in 1886, Marie-Eugène Chevreul, scientist and director of the Gobelin tapestry works, called at the Paris studio of the photographer G. F. Tournachon. A man of ingenuity, Tournachon—better known as the famed "Nadar"—had hit upon a new journalistic idea: the picture interview. Chevreul, an ideal subject, delivered a barrage of controversial opinions on science, evolution, his prescription for a long life (no alcohol—"I am president of the Anjou Society of Wines—but only its honorary president"). The pictures here of Chevreul and Nadar (Nadar's son was at the camera) are from a new book *The Picture History of Photography* by Peter Pollack (Abrams, $17.50). The captions are based on notes taken by a stenographer.

"What shall I write in your album? I see here the name of M. Pasteur. He is one of the great men of our time. Until Pasteur our savants went from known phenomena to the unknown. He reversed the procedure. And I must confess that for years I was one who held this method to be nonsense."

"You know, I don't condemn what I can't explain, but I will say that I *must see*. One is little tempted to lend an ear to inventors, since it is well known that their kind of mind is easily given to illusions. And what is even more important, their conversation is so boring. . . ."

"Mind you, I willingly believe them to be quite sincere. But. . . ."

"I will set down for you my basic philosophical principle. It is not my own, it is by Malebranche. But I have looked a long time and never found a better one."

"One must strive for infallibility without pretending to it."

"Inventors are always inclined to confound invention with imagination, which is not at all the same thing. . . . The inventors of balloons swear to be able to steer them. Let them pick me up at my window and deliver me to the Institute. That way I'll avoid having to descend my staircase."

"As for Mr. Charles Darwin, remember that a single error sows the seed of errors! Me, the son of an orangutan. . . . Never!"

# MIRÓ

By PIERRE SCHNEIDER

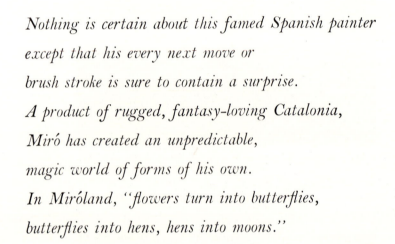

*Nothing is certain about this famed Spanish painter*
*except that his every next move or*
*brush stroke is sure to contain a surprise.*
*A product of rugged, fantasy-loving Catalonia,*
*Miró has created an unpredictable,*
*magic world of forms of his own.*
*In Miróland, "flowers turn into butterflies,*
*butterflies into hens, hens into moons."*

One day in the mid-twenties, Jacques Doucet, a former dictator of Paris fashions and lifetime patron of young writers and artists, was brought to the studio of Joan Miró by two friends of the young Catalan painter—the artist André Masson and the poet Louis Aragon. The elegant old *couturier* sat down, flanked by Masson and Aragon, while Jacques Viot, Miró's dealer, stood in a corner. One after the other, Miró placed his canvases on the easel. The first were still lifes painted in a sharp, crystalline manner derived from cubism. "Quite incisive," M. Doucet commented curtly. But then, as Miró began bringing out painting upon painting from which ordinary reality—even in the fragmented, prismatic version in which the cubists had represented it—had vanished, M. Doucet lapsed into silence. It lasted for an excruciating hour or two. Not until he was in the street again with his two guides did the patron speak up: "Well, my young friends, you have fooled me often, but you won't fool me this time. Your friend is mad, stark mad, and that man in the corner was his keeper. While in there, I said nothing, for fear that he might grow excited. Why, he might have taken his brush and splashed it on my face!"

Three weeks later, Masson met the art patron again. "You know, I have bought two paintings by that friend of

yours," said Doucet. And he added, "I have hung them at the foot of my bed. When I wake up in the morning, I see them, and I am happy for the rest of the day."

Very simply, the aged dress designer had put his finger on the secret of Miró's art and of its appeal: a spontaneous, vivid, fresh elation, instinctively felt and immediately contagious. It is a feeling experienced unconsciously—sometimes even unwillingly—by every spectator. Describing his reaction to Miró's work several years later, the dancer Léonide Massine could only say very nearly the same thing as Jacques Doucet: "When one sees the combination of colors and forms in his pictures, one experiences, quite involuntarily, a joy and an urge to dance."

A painting presented to us is like a window opened on a world. In days past, that window was usually a mere glass pane; behind it, you saw the street, your neighbors, a tree, perhaps distorted or "corrected." Sometimes, the pane would turn into a microscope or a telescope. But Miró was the first artist in history to borrow Alice's looking glass.

What is it we see through his looking glass? To evoke the

*In a Spanish courtyard, Miró displays some of his recent work: ceramic plaques, jugs, and strange objects with his characteristic marks.*

70

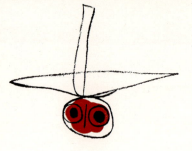

spectacle, we need only close our eyes. Indeed, daylight never rules over Miró's work; even when dozens of phosphorescent suns glow in the painting, its atmosphere remains nocturnal. No wonder, for Miró's world is of the same stuff as dreams are made of. In an endless, vacant landscape defined only by the horizon line, a star sheds a bell-like tear over the misfortunes of a virgin suffering from what appears to be a delicious wound. Is the tear to drop upward or downward? The tear hesitates; happily, a dotted line is there to tell it which way to roll. But I am not telling this story quickly enough: already, everything appears different. "Painting or poetry is made as we make love," says Miró. His personages are hot-blooded, but they have a sense of decency: they do not like to be caught in the act. And so, even while we have been looking, the maiden has turned into a dog—or is it a mushroom?—and the star has extended into a ladder, leading from nowhere to nowhere. "Find flowers that are chairs," the French poet Arthur Rimbaud had asked. For Miró, this is no trouble at all. In his world, flowers turn into butterflies, butterflies into hens, hens into moons—provided they are not all these things at once. They are made of a rubberlike substance endowed with a gift of incessant metamorphosis. What is this gigantic monster? An amoeba. And this infinitesimal dot? A horse.

The denizens of Miróland have another characteristic: their parts are removable and interchangeable. Miró has wrought stranger miracles than the grafting of a kidney. He can replace a kidney by a nose, a belly by a guitar, and a woman's sexual organs by a trolley conductor's purse. He can even make a foot survive indefinitely by itself. All his forms, even the smallest, are filled to the brim with life. At the drop of a hat or of a falling star, they associate, interpenetrate, copulate, procreate at breath-taking speed, and eat or are eaten in complete, rowdy anarchy—an anarchy so profuse and natural that it ends by imposing its own order. All creatures and things are like a myriad of balloons let loose in an exhilarating *Walpurgisnacht*, or better, a "Harlequin's carnival," to borrow Miró's own phrase. A carnival where all is not joy: in the crush, some unfortunate revelers explode, shedding cascades of blood that are immediately lapped up by the rest of the crowd. A grimace may mean either pain or pleasure. One never knows whether one is seeing a comedy or a drama. "Anyway, it amounts to the same thing," says Miró. "Humor is always tragic."

Laughter and torture stem from the same intense, exuberant, unalloyed source. It arises in a realm where sensitivity runs high but sentimentality is unknown. Its inhabitants do not have to sleep in order to dream. They belong to that age which, as La Fontaine wrote, "is without pity": the age of childhood.

For Miró's universe is a cosmic children's corner—on condition that we specify that it was created, not by adults for children, but by the children themselves. If anything, modern psychology has taught us that children do not resemble the edulcorated image grownups have of them. They are innocent, but only in that no sense of guilt accompanies their most improper acts; they are pure, but as undiluted alcohol or vitriol is pure. In the same sense, we can say that the art of Miró is innocent and pure. Just because it is so, it is suffused with eroticism and even sadism. Like children, too, Miró shuns the rational. He concludes alliances with creatures and things that share this trait of not living up to the cold standards of the intellect: with dogs, cats, insects, and plants. Miró shares the child's disregard for proper proportions and relative importance: details that interest him loom large, while elements to which he is indifferent shrink or disappear altogether. (Naturally, the organs by which we satisfy our various senses occupy a preponderant place in his pictures.) No shadow falls between the desire and the realization, between dream and reality, between sky and earth, between night and day.

Perhaps the most striking characteristic of a child's art is that it cannot go wrong. There are no bad drawings by children; in the same way, there are no bad paintings by Miró. The German dramatist Heinrich von Kleist once told the story of a duel between a man and a bear: not only did the animal ward off every thrust of the sword, but he never fell for his opponent's feints—in fact, he seemed not even to suspect them. It is the infallibility of innocence. Miró's color, no matter how free and unpredictable, is always rigorously right, like the acid harmonies of a duck's plumage or a piece of rock. Supremely right, too, is his line, like the flight of a bird, or the patterns made by water spilled from a glass, or the sinuosities of a cowboy's rope about to snare a cow (though in Miró's case, the cow itself may be the lasso).

"For me," says the sculptor Alberto Giacometti, recalling his first impression of Miró's work, "it was the great liberty—something more aerial, more disengaged, lighter than anything I had ever seen. In a way, it was absolutely perfect. Miró could not make a spot without making it fall right. He was so truly a painter that all he needed was to drop three blobs of color on the canvas for it to exist and be coherent as a painting."

"Truly a painter": this, of course, is what distinguishes Miró from the child. Indeed, there lies the source of a profound conflict. For painting is an adult activity. It is not surprising, therefore, that the realm of childhood is usually forbidden ground to artists. When they trespass upon it, they become childish, not childlike. That is the reason for Miró's secret, for the elation that is so specifically his own. Even more fully than Paul Klee, whom he acknowledges as "one of my family," Miró has placed a mature skill at the disposal of a primitive imagination. And this unique conjunction has reopened for us the road to what Baudelaire called

*The Miró family farm at Montroig on the Catalonian mainland provided subject matter for* The Farm, *painted in 1921-22 during Miró's early phase of development. Its owner is Ernest Hemingway.*

*Left, the artist below a decorated, glazed stone at the farm of his ceramic collaborator, Artigas; center, decorating a live cactus; right, playing with Artigas and his son behind facelike plaques.*

the green paradises of childhood.

In appearance, nothing could stand in greater contrast to Miró's work than Miró himself. His art is extravagant; the man is the incarnation of propriety and sobriety. Correct in dress, quiet in behavior, meticulous in his routines, he resembles less an artist in the popular conception than a good bourgeois. To anyone who knows Miró's painting, the opposition is almost comically startling, though the humor is always perfectly unintentional—for Miró, even in his most exuberant fancies, remains grave. Like children, he plays, but his games are in dead earnest.

However, the discrepancy between man and work is apparent, not real. Actually, nothing could be more logical than Miró's good conduct. As the depository of a fragile treasure—a childlike purity in a world of grownups—he knows that he must take pains to preserve it. The best method? Ask your son or daughter. They will tell you that the way to avoid encroachment by adults is to pretend to be playing their game. Say hello and thank you nicely, pass the butter, answer when spoken to, and throw the anxious art critic an occasional maxim that will sate his curiosity. Behind that demure façade your mind can take off unhampered toward Mars or the moon.

One of Miró's surrealist companions recalls having been invited to the farm of Miró's parents, at Montroig, in Catalonia. "There's just one little thing," Miró told him; "for the sake of the people there, you'll have to go to church on Sunday." This, for a surrealist, was tantamount to recantation. But Miró hastened to add: "Don't worry. We'll go up to the balcony and eat watermelons."

Throughout his career, Miró has been eating watermelons in the balcony. He has raised the art of affable noncommitment to the point of perfection. Events, aesthetic and otherwise, do affect Miró and his art, to be sure, yet tangentially and in unforeseeable ways. He accepts from external influences only what fits into his own concerns, and with an unerring, instinctive shrewdness he steers clear of all that might upset his equilibrium. His favorite defense is silence. Miró's silences are legendary. A friend of his tells that he had been with him for hours, without Miró's opening his mouth. At last, in desperation, the friend asked: "What do you think of Verdaguer [one of Catalonia's better known modern poets, mention of whose name is bound to provoke an enthusiastic response from his compatriots]?" Miró gravely replied: "And you?"

The fruit of this shrewd obstinacy is clear: as Masson put it, "He has remained completely intact." Not even time has been able to dent Miró's small, compact, solid figure. Today, he looks much as he did as a boy: the square face has become rounder, the hair has grayed, but the same smile plays on the thin, pressed lips, and the same small, alert eyes scrutinize the world for signs of connivance that remain invisible to the rest of us.

Childhood is Miró's secret, but it was not until he was a man of thirty that he discovered it. Before then, his course pointed, or at least seemed to point, in quite a different direction. He was born on April 20, 1893, the son of a goldsmith whose father, in turn, was a blacksmith. From them, Joan inherited a love for artisanship, for well-made objects in the folk tradition. He was born in the Pasaje de Credito, a narrow street in the old quarter of Barcelona, but—then as later—spent much time on the family farm at Montroig near Tarragona, "a brutal place," as Miró says, "raw to the point of grandiosity." His mother came from a family of well-to-do tradespeople in Palma, the capital of Majorca. The gentle delicacy of Majorca contrasts with the explosive violence of Montroig. Both influences are present in Miró's work from the start; together, they furnish its basic co-ordinates. Recently, Miró confided to his neighbor and friend, the distinguished Spanish novelist Camilo José Cela: "Until I shall have managed to reconcile the power of Montroig with the delicacy of Majorca, I shall not have become a mature artist."

From 1907 to 1910, Miró went to the School of Fine Arts in Barcelona, where the teaching was resolutely academic. But Miró was not at home in the classroom and proved to be a mediocre student. Color came to him naturally, but form—conventional, modeled form, that is—eluded him. Finally his parents pulled him out of school and forced him to take a job as a clerk. After two years, during which Miró ceased to paint, he went back to art school for another try. He remembers himself at this time as "a monument of clumsiness." To hammer a sense of volume into his head, his teachers forced him to draw objects, after having felt their surfaces with eyes closed. After three years of this diet, Miró left the school, still a hesitant beginner.

Help came from outside. In 1915, an exhibit of post-impressionist painting was brought from Paris to the Dalmau Gallery in Barcelona. The man who made the deepest impression on Miró was Van Gogh, no doubt because his simplifications, distortions, and brutal straightforwardness struck a familiar chord. These were precisely the qualities Miró had already noticed and responded to in the frescoes decorating the Romanesque churches of his native Catalonia.

To Barcelona, the art dealer Dalmau also introduced Fauvism, which had emancipated color from literal realism, and cubism, which had emancipated form. Aware that his shortcomings lay primarily in the domain of form, Miró adopted the discipline of cubism to strengthen the bones of his compositions. Yet Miró could not keep up the discipline of rigid composition for long. Not even the heaviest contour could prevent reality as he saw it from escaping its noose. There are strangely anarchic parts in these early, deliberate pictures of his. In them, nature bulges and sways ominously; a thigh suddenly becomes inflated, like a balloon about to rise out of the canvas. These works have some of the frustrated fury of Van Gogh. They are powerful, moving

A dream studio for creating a dream world: in this building at Palma on the island of Majorca, recently designed for him by José Luis Sert, Miró does most of his work. Below, the artist stands in his main studio, sheltered by overhangs and louvered windows against the strong Mediterranean light. A smaller upstairs room is used for print-making, to which Miró devotes a large share of time. Around him he has gathered a collection of engaging natural and man-made objects, such as those grouped at right.

75

failures—failures that Miró attributed to the fact that reality still eluded him.

So he tried another way to ensnare it. After Montroig, Majorca now had its say. In 1918, his draftsmanship became painstakingly precise and linear: every detail was reproduced with a delicate exactitude reminiscent both of naïve art and of Persian miniatures. In 1919, too, Miró made his first trip to Paris, and in 1920 he moved there, though he continued to spend his summers at Montroig. He was still engaged on his fastidious inventory of nature's contents. Yet the things to be enumerated were infinite in number. You began with a nude woman, and you might never get beyond the butterfly embroidered on the hassock on which she sat. Miró worked more and more slowly, producing at most three or four pictures a year. It was a discouraging business, all the more since reality seemed to freeze into a pillar of salt the moment he looked at it. In 1922 Miró had reached a dead end; in an ultimate attempt to capture reality, he painted *The Farm* (reproduced on page 73).

*The Farm* is a compendium, a *summa* of all that mattered most to Miró: here Montroig lies exposed in the merciless, analytical light of Catalonia that omits nothing, complete from the snail in the furrow to the crack in the wall. It took Miró nine months to execute *The Farm*, which Ernest Hemingway acquired shortly after. It was an ending, but also a beginning. All the elements that we encounter later in emancipation, are present here, but still shackled. It was as if Miró had unconsciously compiled the glossary of a language which he was soon to speak. By 1924 the decisive step had been taken: Miró painted *The Tilled Field*. It is Montroig all over again, the essential ingredients are identical but they have suffered a sea change—as our familiar surroundings do when they appear to us in dreams. Something had happened: Miró had found his road to Damascus.

That road, for him, passed through the Rue Blomet, where he rented a studio in a decrepit house at Number 45. The house was condemned, but it was reprieved long enough for "objective hazard"—the surrealists' name for Providence—to intervene. By chance, another young painter, André Masson, had rented the studio next to Miró's. The furious disorder of Masson's atelier contrasted strangely with the im-

*Stirred in the twenties by the new school of surrealism, Miró turned away from natural scenes and painted such spontaneous visions as the strangely naïve and poetic* Dog Barking at the Moon (left). *In 1940, in quite another mood, he painted in tempera* The Poetess (above), *a gay design in which the viewer can identify a few of the swirling objects as birds and eyes, but may have difficulty identifying a poetess.*

77

maculate cleanliness of Miró's. "Going from the one to the other was like passing from a novel by Dostoevsky to a tale by the Comtesse de Ségur," remembers a writer who frequently visited them. Through Masson, Miró discovered surrealism.

It would be more exact to say that through surrealism, Miró discovered himself. It was as if he suddenly had heard spoken aloud the thoughts he had not even dared to formulate in silence. André Breton's *Manifesto of Surrealism* of 1924 proclaimed the legitimacy of the revolt against reason, extolled the inviolability of imagination, and asserted the superiority of unconscious over conscious activity. Against the sublime, surrealism set up the subliminal. Primitives, madmen—all those who had not cut themselves off from the pure source of irrationality—were vindicated. "There are fairy tales to be written for grownups," Breton wrote. Miró must have thought that these words were addressed especially to him. Be a dreamer, the surrealist doctrine preached, and it added: be a child. "The man who plunges into surrealism exaltedly re-experiences the best part of his childhood." Miró's later work, with its startling juxtapositions and continuous transformations, was to be a constant illustration of the psychoanalytic principle adopted by the surrealists: free association. Here was the way out of the prismatic prison of cubism. "I shall break the guitars," Miró announced. Surrealism provided him with the tools. For less talented artists, surrealism was an end; for Miró, it constituted a means—a kind of calisthenics to reactivate spiritual muscles that had become atrophied through idleness.

But liberty did not come at once. In paintings like *The Tilled Field* (1923-24) the old elements are not replaced but simply rearranged—taken apart, shuffled, and recomposed. Gradually, however, the actors are set into motion by free association, a step forward that no naïve painter has ever been able to take: the naïve can only add things, and Miró has learned to multiply them. Strange creatures begin to appear, frightening even to their creator. To make them acceptable, Miró turned them into toys: a key is stuck into them to permit winding. Soon, however, Miró was seized altogether by the new forces that he had deliberately unleashed. Picture upon picture was now swiftly completed. In them, the fresh, unheard-of universe that has made Miró famous was born.

Yet surrealism does not imply, in Miró's case, repudiating reality. Far from it. The first time he showed a painting to the poet Paul Eluard, the latter exclaimed: "Oh, what a pretty sun!" "It's a potato," Miró replied, obviously vexed. Miró is not one of those timid visionaries who can dream only with their eyes closed. *Miro* in Spanish means "I look." Miró absorbs the spectacle of the outside world with avidity, although he does not see it with quite the same eyes as the ordinary mortal of the technological age. He is prompt to discern that wandering and always elusive point at which

reality—any reality—turns into magic.

This aptitude for grasping the magic lurking within reality is a fundamental characteristic of Catalonia and its people. It is in Barcelona or Montroig that we encounter the spirit and the ingredients of Miró's art at grass-roots level. He has never ceased feeding on them. During his Parisian period, in a deeply symbolic gesture, he had taken with him, at the time of *The Farm*, dried tufts of grass from Montroig. His yearly pilgrimage to Catalonia was more than just a holiday. There he found the atmosphere that, as he says, is capital to him. In spite of the durably dampening effect of the Civil War and its tragic outcome, even the casual visitor cannot fail to detect, in Barcelona, the elements of Miró's world in the raw. Everywhere the ancient, ineradicable, popular spirit manifests itself with vivid immediacy and an almost expressionist violence. Fantasy and anarchy run wild in the interiors of shops piled high with sausages, hams, and extravagantly shaped bottles. No distinction is drawn between the real and the false: in the park of the Ciudadela a sturdy fence surrounds a life-size, cement mammoth; the sculptured Moor's head hanging from the organ in the Barcelona cathedral has a real beard; in a glove shop, live birds peck at imitation apples. Trivial spectacles? Not to Miró. Once some of his Parisian friends had urged a lady archaeologist eager to study Catalan art to look him up. She came back outraged: after announcing to her that he would take her to see the most important sights in Barcelona, he had made her walk all the way through town to show her the hooks and artificial flies in a fishing store, and then all the way across again to contemplate some preposterously mauve pants in a tailor's window.

In the realm of art, Miró's earliest and most lasting impression was provided by the frescoes of medieval Catalonia, now conveniently gathered in the Museum of Catalan Art. The same basic local features are clearly evident in these Romanesque works: a brutal straightforwardness of statement often bordering on the grotesque, the cartoonlike. Their content too is typically Catalan with its jocose cruelty and the ability of its forms to interplay and to transform indefinitely. Hell and the Apocalypse were, of course, favorite themes for the artists. We meet men sizzling in the caldron, and a host of other ingenious tortures. An executioner jig-saws his victim from head to toe, and both seem equally delighted by the pretty zigzag pattern traced by the blade. The air is thick with flying devils and angels, roving stars and fishtail doves. A dog sports eyes on his back; a man displays a vulture's head; and even the letter *epsilon* may change into a bird in flight.

This violent, indigenous fancy found an eminently suitable outlet in the direct, expressive idiom provided by the Romanesque style. The Gothic, on the other hand, stifled it with its carefully weighed, meticulous intellectuality, as did the succession of styles evolved out of the Renaissance. This points to the central predicament of Catalan art: its

CONTINUED ON PAGE 126

Highly personal as it is, Miró's art nevertheless reflects his environment. His free and exuberant forms bear a resemblance to the work of the noted Catalan architect Antonio Gaudí, who early in this century built such startling structures as that at left—a Barcelona apartment house fronted with swaying curves and treelike shapes. Other motifs that find their echo in Miró are the rugged mountains of Montserrat near Barcelona (below, left), where otherworldly pinnacles overshadow the old monastery. A direct influence on him was exerted by Catalan folk art dating back to the Middle Ages, with its mixture of the naïve, the religious, and the brutal—as exemplified below in a painting of the martyrdom of Saint Juliet, done on wood in about the year 1100.

*OVERLEAF:*

Working in still another medium—color lithography—Miró in 1957 produced this startling conception entitled Femme au Miroir. With his love of bold line and hard, posterlike colors, the artist has turned increasingly in recent years to print-making, and is outstanding today in the fields of lithography, woodcuts, aquatints, and etchings. Pursuing his ceramic interests at the same time, he designed two tiled murals for the new UNESCO building in Paris that in 1958 won the $10,000 Guggenheim International Award.

# WHAT
# NOT
# TO
# SEE
# IN
# EUROPE

Spring is here again, and with it the annual flood of glamourous travel literature telling Americans Where to Go and What to See. The prospective American traveler is showered with promises of glorified sights abroad, tempted by pictures of enchanting women in enchanting landscapes, fascinated by full-page ads of Technicolor sunsets. There is just one thing missing in this bewitching setup: some sound advice to the eager wanderer on Where Not to Go and What Not to See.

As tourists, Americans are pretty much like people elsewhere: filled with healthy curiosity, endowed with pardonable gullibility, driven by fierce determination not to miss the Big Show. The lure of the unknown, smartly exploited by the supersalesmen of tourism, makes children out of sophisticates and enthusiasts out of misanthropes. New Yorkers who at home wouldn't dream of going near Radio City Music Hall ("That's strictly for tourists, Mac") run up the stairs of Paris' Eiffel Tower. And I know at least one worldly Parisian *boulevardier* who never goes to Montmartre ("*C'est seulement pour les touristes, mon vieux*") but was on the top of the Empire State Building an hour after his arrival in New York.

Tourism also has its more ludicrous aspects, whose villains are armies of Madison Avenue advertising men, travel agency conspirators, night-club operators, salesmen

of sin, and sundry promoters of mechanized fun. But tourism is going to stay with us forever, like the income tax. This, in the opinion of at least one veteran observer, stresses the need for an occasional offside comment on What to Leave Unseen—at least on the second time around.

As I assume that you have already made your arrangements for the Grand Tour of Europe—all-expense, predigested, go-now-pay-later, personally guided or whatnot —I have little hope that you may be influenced by my discommendations. In tourism and love a man never learns from the mistakes of others; he has got to find out for himself—and has to pay for it. But at least you cannot say that you haven't been warned.

My discommendations are of necessity highly subjective, a reflection of my personal prejudices. One man's Beaujolais is another man's poison. The Grand Tour of Europe is like a modern painting: it's interesting but people can't always agree exactly why. My suggestions are mainly for the traveler who cares more about content than appearance. If you want to know more about the people than about the specialties of the place, you are my audience. I may not win friends but perhaps I will influence some readers.

You will not find me counseling you to avoid certain countries altogether. There exist irritating national traits— gypping in France, tipping in Austria, suspicion in the

*By* JOSEPH WECHSBERG

Soviet Union—but despite what superpatriots may say, there are no objectionable nations.

My pet aversions are based on repeated experiences over a long period of time, not on isolated incidents. I wouldn't black-list a restaurant because I once had a bad meal there; maybe it was the chef's day off. It's a different story after a dozen bad meals. Instead of giving the names of certain hotels, restaurants, or travel institutions that I intend to bypass from now on, I'm giving you generic facts. Draw your own conclusions. In this game the reader is expected to do a little homework. Constructive criticism is the keynote of this report which I present as a public service with malice toward none.

The American tourist's trip to Europe is often organized down to the last half-hour. There is no time for improvisation, surprise, introspection. The client must be on the go all the time. If you were bored for ten minutes, your trip, like a Broadway show, is considered a flop. Togetherness has become the symbol—and the curse—of modern tourism. No one should think for himself. Groups of docile sheep are herded through revolving doors into hotel lobbies, sent up the mountains in cable cars, channeled into opera houses, told to attend Tyrolean Nights. Hurry, hurry! The next sight-seeing bus is already waiting. You are hot, tired, crowded; even sardines would revolt against such a life. *Kultur* is disseminated in concentrated doses. Every night the sights are checked off like items on a laundry list.

Generally, my discommendations fall into four categories.

First, the snobbish, fashionable, 3-*O* places—Overdone, Overcrowded, Overcharging. Capri and Ischia in Italy, Cannes and St. Tropez in France, Kitzbühel and Zürs in Austria, Garmisch and Berchtesgaden in Germany belong in this group. When everybody who is anybody begins to talk about these places, the wise traveler knows he had better stay away.

Second, places where scenic beauty and native charm have been ruined by commercial tourism. The châteaux of the Loire, the wine villages along the German Rhine, Volendam in Holland, Killarney in Ireland, the Zugspitze and the Jungfraujoch in the Alps, Sorrento and Amalfi in southern Italy are tourist meccas that ought to be avoided.

Third, the brash, vulgar, uninhibited tourist traps set for the exploitation of the unsuspecting sucker: Paris' Montmartre, Hamburg's Reeperbahn, Munich's *Oktoberfest*, Belgium's *Carnival de Binche*, and most summer festivals.

And fourth, the 3-*D* places—Dull, Dreary, Depressing—where you're likely to ask yourself, "What the hell am I doing here?" A few places come to the mind almost automatically: Birmingham and Liverpool, Lille and Rennes, Frankfurt am Main and Bonn, Salonika and the modern districts of Athens, Switzerland's Bern and the Netherlands' The Hague. And, above all, the tired, gray, cheerless cities in most Iron Curtain countries—in case you plan to go there.

It is an unwritten law among the salesmen of local color that American travelers like their sights well scrubbed, wrapped in cellophane. In the Burgundy district of France you are taken to sumptuous establishments with indirect lights in the pompous cellars of the big shippers of Beaune and Dijon; you are offered a glass of second-rate wine and a piece of first-rate promotion literature. If you really care to find out about the people who make the wine, don't stay in the big cellars. Go to the dreamy, sun-drenched villages and talk to the men in the vineyards. Stay away from the big firms whose names appear on the billboards and talk to the hard-working guys with blue aprons.

A good general rule: avoid all famous tourist places in the middle of the season. Venice in July is a midsummer nightmare; overcrowded hotels, deplorable service, doubled prices. The *Kitsch* trade flourishes. In the back yards skilled little crooks manufacture "antiques."

Nothing, I once thought, would ever spoil the French Riviera for me, but I didn't count with prosperity, the small car, and Mlles Bardot and Sagan. Certain stretches of the celebrated Côte d'Azur are now vast camping sites filled with noise and soda pop bottles, inhabited by amateur photographers in search of pretty girls and not-so-pretty girls in search of anybody. Headwaiters talk to you only after hard currency bribes, and cashiers make out their bills by multiplication. Reception managers have permanently lifted eyebrows from constant disapproval of customers. The charm and beauty are gone for a while. Not recommended as long as the current boom lasts.

In Switzerland you are told you *must* go up to the Jungfraujoch. Over 11,000 feet altitude. Europe's highest cog railway. Breath-taking panorama. So you get up at dawn, ride in a crowded bus to Lauterbrunnen, in a crowded cog railway to the Jungfraujoch, stand in line to buy a post card, to go to the rest room, to look into a telescope, to get some food, to see the panorama (if you were lucky and the day turned out to be clear), and then you go down again in various crowded conveyances. You will be relieved when it's all over and you can check off another Must. For the money you spent you might have seen three less famous but more rewarding mountaintops.

Still, it only takes a day. A winter vacation in Kitzbühel or Zürs, Arosa or Davos takes longer. Sartorially minded skiers who change their costume three times a day and who care more about dry martinis in the bar than about dry-powder snow on the slopes will love it there. Their room may be tiny but it doesn't matter since they spend the night in the bar and the day on the slopes. After three weeks of such a vacation they often need another vacation to relax. There are places in the Alps which are regular bus terminals during the "high" season but beautiful in May or October: Austria's Zell am See, Italy's Val Gardena, Switzerland's Engadine.

Paris, the City of Light and the unrivaled Number One Place on every conducted tour of Europe, offers many Things Not to See. Thus, the Eiffel Tower (except for amateur photographers); a night at the Opéra (a pompous mausoleum with an apathetic orchestra and second-rate singers); the Latin Quarter, which has changed since Henry Murger wrote *Scènes de la Vie de Bohème;* and Montmartre, the world's most celebrated tourist trap.

Thirty years ago, when I was a pale-faced fiddler in the disreputable *boîtes de nuit* around Place Pigalle, the virtuosi of the art of gypping still had their professional ethics. Champagne was expensive but at least it was genuine. Today you pay sixteen dollars for a bottle of *vin mousseux* whose label is hidden in a silver bucket. You would think only fools wish to dine around Place Pigalle, where the food is less good and more expensive than elsewhere in town; but even wise people don't mind being fools once in a while, particularly on their first trip to Paris. And if your researches deal with the Body Beautiful, you may be in for serious financial trouble. It's safer to go to the regular show at the Folies-Bergère. Beautiful women with no G strings attached; you know what you get, at fixed prices.

For connoisseurs of Atlantic City and Coney Island there are bush-league Montmartres all over Europe. Munich's *Oktoberfest* is an exhaustive study in noise and vulgarity, beer and belching. Hospitality of a robust sort is offered all year long at Munich's Hofbräuhaus. Former habitués of the Minsky circuit should not miss the Reeperbahn in the St. Pauli suburb of Hamburg. It is noisier than New Orleans' Mardi gras, but less sexy than an American strip tease. The Germans do not know that an undressed girl is less attractive than a half-dressed one.

We are now approaching the borderline zone of not-so-good taste where Everything Goes. The staid city of Basel, Switzerland, takes on an off-limits character every year during its *Fastnacht*. And Düsseldorf, Cologne, and Mainz —utterly respectable communities during most of the year —turn into a bacchanal during the annual carnival which makes brothers out of people who normally can't stand one another. Recommended only to amateurs of Uninhibited Fun.

Professional merrymakers and congenital sentimentalists should not miss Vienna's *Heuriger*—the small suburban inns and wine gardens where the new wine is drunk all year long. It tastes like clear spring water but isn't, as devotees have found out the morning after on waking up with a colossal hangover. Fortunately Alka-Seltzer is now available in Vienna. You bring your own food, friends, and fun to the *Heuriger*. In no time everybody is singing, hugging, and fraternizing. It's great fun the first time, but repeated visits dull the pleasure. You may discover that your neighbors are not quite as *gemütlich* as they appear to the unskilled eye. It is recommended to avoid political discussions and criticism of Vienna and the Viennese, and don't walk off with somebody else's wife. Sometimes a new-wine party winds up in an old court building. The waiter sometimes adds the date—say "12/11"—or his weight, in kilos, to the figure on the bill, but no one minds. You are only middle-aged once.

Summer festivals are a more serious matter; many of them are carefully organized, state-supported rackets whose main purpose is to relieve the innocent tourist painlessly of all excess cash. Richard Wagner's festival in Bayreuth and

Max Reinhardt's in Salzburg were beautiful ideas: to give dedicated lovers of music and the arts fine performances in perfect surroundings. But since the end of the last war, festivals have become big business. Many are run by promoters who know little about the arts. I still go to Bayreuth to watch Richard Wagner's grandsons create their magnificent renaissance of the Old Master's work, but I go there during rehearsals, before the fanfares and the high-priced fun start. When the black Mercedes 300's arrive on the Hügel, disgorging overfed *Wirtschaftswunder* magnates and overdressed women, it's time to leave. During the long intermission they drink oceans of bad *Sekt* and eat mountains of mayonnaise eggs.

The festival malaise has affected even Salzburg, once a lovely baroque dream town and now a sort of large jukebox presenting Mozart music as well as Mozart cakes, Mozart chocolate candies, Mozart gimcracks, and Mozart music boxes. There are still beautiful moments in Salzburg—an evening at the Residenz in good weather, *The Marriage of Figaro* in any weather, a Mozart Mass at a local church— but too often the Mozart harmonies are marred by the scratching sounds of ball pens on American Express traveler's checks.

And farther south, in Aix-en-Provence—a Cézanne painting come to life—taxi drivers refuse to give you back the change, and honest chefs water their soups because at festival time *ces imbéciles* will swallow anything. The Roman arena of Verona (and similar *al fresco* productions) will delight music lovers who think highly of Grand Central Station during the rush hour. The musical standards are almost as good as at the Hollywood Bowl, and the merry bedlam is even better. Performances last into the early morning hours. By the time you have managed to locate your car and come back to your hotel, it will be dawn—which saves you a night of bad sleep in the oppressive heat. The mosquitoes are vicious and the windows have no screens. Still, this is known in some circles as a Perfect Holiday.

Nostalgia seekers ought to be warned. Revisiting the places of your early memories, it has been observed, often ends in disappointment. Ex-student princes who go back to the idyllic Heidelberg of their youthful days will find a noisy, crowded American Army headquarters town, as peaceful as a roller coaster stadium. Other deceptions on the rocky road to nostalgia are Portofino, the Lake Garda spots of Riva and Gardone, Bordighera and Rapallo on the Italian Riviera, and Monte Carlo. What happened to that once so lovely operetta town? The old gentlemen with white spats and the black-hatted old ladies are gone, and their Rolls Royces are now used as taxicabs. Celebrity hunters crowd the streets of Beausoleil and the little *bistros* in La Condamine, where prosperous proprietors have installed chromium chairs and imitation-leather seats.

Many American travelers nowadays consider their epicurean discoveries more important than bargain-hunting expeditions or their excursions into the jungles of the libido. Gastronomic guidebooks, pseudo-epicurean societies, and self-appointed experts take advantage of this trend. They tell the customers where and what to eat. These recommendations are more often given by high-pressure salesmen than by low-pressure gastronomes.

Personally I try to avoid restaurants that thrive on the ignorance of their snobbish clientele. The names of these places can be gathered from the current society columns. The guests in these restaurants are less concerned with the quality of their dishes than with the position of their tables. The headwaiters are pompous and the waiters are waspish. Some restaurateurs run a profitable side line supplying airlines with precooked "gourmet" food, delivered in metal containers, like lubrication grease. Others sell *sauce Périgourdine* and *crêpes Suzette* in cans. Such nutritional workshops should not be confused with good restaurants.

I once wrote that a guidebook telling people Where Not to Eat would be as welcome for travelers with delicate stomachs as the invaluable *Guide Michelin*. Since then some of my best friends in the restaurant trade haven't talked to me, which encourages me to go on with my researches on behalf of the sensitive palate. Generally I bypass restaurants that advertise (good restaurants just don't do it); restaurants where the food is heavily spiced and extravagantly garnished to conceal the mediocrity of its ingredients; restaurants that don't buy fresh butter but hire fresh fiddlers who surround your table while the bill is presented; restaurants specializing in pyrotechnical cuisine where every second dish is served with flames; and restaurants where the cooking is

CONTINUED ON PAGE 120

*By* ROBERT EMMETT GINNA

# The Tree of Coole

*The great age of Irish literature is commemorated in Lady Gregory's garden*

In the ruined garden the copper beech tree stands, majestic as a sentinel at the last tattoo. Its bark bears many weathered marks—man-made carvings of initials, names, and seals. Many famous hands fashioned these. For we are in the presence of the Tree of Irish Letters, and can read on its bark a short history of Ireland's literary renaissance.

Here stood the House of Coole. Only the gutted shells of some outbuildings stand now, and the high wall enclosing the garden. Once this place knew graciousness and gaiety. It was a great house and its owners were loved and respected in the neighborhood. No caller was ever turned away from its door. Today there is nothing left, nothing to mark that door through which passed Ireland's greatest writers. For Coole was a focus for Irish culture in the early decades of this century. To it came the men who carried Ireland's literature around the world; they came to gather about the hearth of Lady Augusta Gregory.

Only the copper beech tree recalls that past. Visitors to Coole would stroll in the garden with Lady Gregory and pause to make their mark upon the silver-gray trunk of the beech. The great tree is their memorial.

Lady Gregory was born Isabella Augusta Persse in 1852 at Roxboro' Hall, not many miles from Coole. In 1881 she wed Sir William Henry Gregory, who had been a member of Parliament and a notable governor of Ceylon. Coole Park had been in his old Cromwellian family since 1768. With her marriage, Lady Gregory acquired the fierce love for the lands of Coole that was to be one of the two consuming passions of her life. The other was to be the Abbey Theatre.

Sir William was many years Lady Gregory's senior, and he died in 1892. With William Butler Yeats, Edward Martyn, and George Moore, Lady Gregory founded the Irish Literary Theatre seven years later. By 1904 it had evolved into the Abbey Theatre, and Lady Gregory had released her energy into writing plays and books. Until her death, in 1932, she remained a director of the Abbey and its real bulwark. She served and supported it in every way, from sewing costumes to shepherding it through its tumultuous American tour of 1911, when J. M. Synge's *The Playboy of the Western World* offended the Irish-Americans as a crude smear on their origin—the company being arrested in Philadelphia for performing "immoral or indecent plays." She offered the quiet and hospitality of Coole to many writers, and, master or journeyman, they came.

The preservation of Coole was the trial of Lady Gregory's life. Its land never brought much income and she struggled throughout her years to keep the estate intact, its great woods and lakes a sanctuary of the kind that was disappearing from Ireland. Holding on against taxes and the general pressure against the Protestant, landholding "Anglo-Irish," she noted in her journal on August 1, 1921: "For Ireland's sake also I keep it. I think the country would be poorer without Coole."

After her husband's death, the man who most shared Lady Gregory's love for Coole was William Butler Yeats. That proud and pensive man walked through its seven woods and listened in the dusk to the medley of chimes he could strike from the huge bell-rock by the lake shore. He lay and watched the wild swans rise and beat across the lake, and, better than any other man could, he set down forever the haunting mood of Coole in his books of poems, *The Wild Swans at Coole* and *In the Seven Woods*. While walking through the stands of ash and oak, beech and fir, with the barking of foxes upon the air and the hazel wands flickering through the leaves, it was not hard for Yeats to hear the age-old voices and the hot cries out of history. The seven woods were vast and Yeats was once lost in them, as was George Bernard Shaw on another occasion. Shaw was missing for hours and had to be sought by men on horseback in the night.

Neither love nor loyalty could save Coole in the end. Slowly it was parceled off. In 1927 the house and land were sold to the Ministry of Lands and Agriculture, although Lady Gregory was able to lease the house, gardens, and lawns at £100 yearly until her death.

By this time many of the great landed families had been driven from their estates by taxation, by the pressure of land reform acts, or by the terrorism of the Irish Republican Army against families that were Protestant and Anglo-Irish. Predominantly these families were fiercely, loyally Irish. As for Lady Gregory, she described herself in 1928 as "a 'rebel' with the Nationalists all through—more than they know or my nearest realized." Still, Roxboro' Hall, her own family's home, was burned by the Irish Republican Army. The House of Coole was to be torn down by the Free State government.

It is not clear why this happened. After the auction of the furnishings—Lady Gregory before her death had sold much of the fine library piecemeal to support the place—the Free State Forestry Department spent some money in renovating the house. One of the Persse family was interested in taking over the house at this time, but it was ordered to be demolished.

The House of Coole was approached through an avenue of ilex trees. They are there yet, a Gothic vault of twining green. Beyond, where the drive curved to a door opening on laughter and good cheer, there is emptiness—a meadow with cattle grazing. Silence, save for the cattle lowing and the flutter of birds. A path leads through a row of firs down to that strange river and the lake which rises and falls suddenly. On it the wild swans still sail by scores. Overhead they fly, wheeling low now over the dark water, giving those wild cries that made the poet's heart leap.

A splintered gate, sagging between tall stone pillars, marks the garden. It is wild and almost claimed by the encroaching wood. Stray flowers pluck their way up through the snarl of brush. Far in the garden and over everything towers the beech tree, deep copper-bronze except beneath its branches where the undersides of the leaves are green and the light floods through them with cathedral hues. Around the trunk the Forestry Department has erected a crude wire fence, topped with barbed wire.

The bark is scored by many knives. Many of the initials are those of authors lost to memory; others are easier to place. There is the Æ, in triangle—colophon of George Russell, the bearded poet, editor, and seer. There are the initials of William Butler Yeats and his artist brother, Jack.

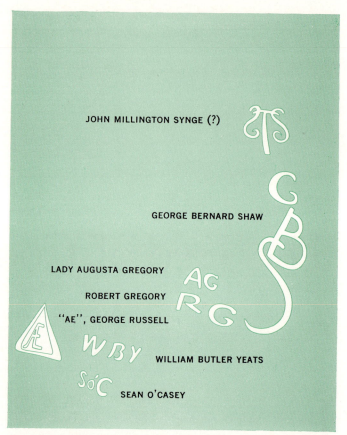

JOHN MILLINGTON SYNGE (?)

GEORGE BERNARD SHAW

LADY AUGUSTA GREGORY

ROBERT GREGORY

"AE", GEORGE RUSSELL

WILLIAM BUTLER YEATS

SEAN O'CASEY

*Key shows location on trunk of some of the most famous initials.*

Beneath is the S O'C of Sean O'Casey, who was still working as a laborer and writing plays when Lady Gregory invited him to Coole. The R G is that of Robert, Lady Gregory's son, the flier whose death Yeats eulogized in a beautiful lyric. High up, the lyre-like monogram is thought to be the mark of John Millington Synge, the Abbey genius, who died young after a short career as a playwright. And lo, like Abou Ben Adhem's, the great linked G B S leads all the rest, larger and grander.

Deciphering the tree is a game which every visitor must surely play. Many of the foremost artists of their time traced their stay at Coole upon this tree. There are initials that are not readily found, but must be here—George Moore's, Augustus John's, Oliver St. John Gogarty's, and Lennox Robinson's, to name a few. They were all at Coole. It is not easy to find the letters among those which vandals have added.

Still, the tree of Coole stands. Reading the letters incised on it, the traveler knows a little more of that furious outburst when Ireland's artists looked into their hearts and heritage and gave to English literature one of its great epochs. Their work is their monument. Yet the great beech endures as a memorial to the doughty lady who loved this land and, believing in Ireland's artists, drew them together at the House of Coole.

*Robert Emmett Ginna produced and directed the* Wisdom *series on NBC Television, and has written for* Life, Look, *and other magazines.*

*"The Smith of Smiths."*
LORD MACAULAY

*"A fellow of infinite fun (if not much humour) and of a fine digestion and some sense."*
THOMAS CARLYLE

*"I have a superstitious veneration for the cloth, which his free-and-easy wearing of it occasionally disturbs a little."*
FANNY KEMBLE BUTLER

*"A more profligate parson I never met."*
GEORGE IV

*"Sydney at breakfast made me actually cry with laughing. I was obliged to start up from the table."*
THOMAS MOORE

SYDNEY SMITH

*"The loudest wit I e'er was deafened with."*
GEORGE GORDON BYRON

*"He drew such a ludicrous caricature . . . that Sir James Mackintosh rolled on the floor in fits of laughter."*
LORD JOHN RUSSELL

*"I wish you would tell Mr. Sydney Smith that of all the men I ever heard of and never saw, I have the greatest curiosity to see and the greatest interest to know him."*
CHARLES DICKENS

*"Now I shall be able to do something for Sydney Smith."*
CHARLES GREY
(ON BECOMING PRIME MINISTER)

*"I sat next to Sydney Smith, who was delightful . . . I don't remember a more agreeable party."*
BENJAMIN DISRAELI

*"An odd mixture of Punch and Cato."*
MARQUESS OF LANSDOWNE

*"He is a very clever fellow, but he will never be a bishop."*
GEORGE III

# "The Greatest Wit in England"

*So the critic Jeffrey dubbed Sydney Smith, the exuberant Anglican divine,*

*Whig publicist, iconoclast, and bon vivant who flourished from the time*

*of George III well into that of Victoria and knew practically everybody*

*By* HESKETH PEARSON

A man who could make so decorous a person as Sarah Siddons forget that she was a tragedy queen and send her into paroxysms of laughter, was clearly a person of note. But Sydney Smith, one of the most irrepressible and colorful figures of late Georgian and early Victorian England, has other claims to our attention. He was the first to realize that one could only quicken an Englishman's intelligence by tickling his sense of humor. By making his countrymen laugh he made them think, in which respect he was the spiritual ancestor of Oscar Wilde and Bernard Shaw.

Sydney Smith had little to say about his ancestors. His grandfather, he told Walter Scott, "disappeared about the time of the assizes, and we asked no questions." He further informed an expert in heraldry that "the Smiths never had any arms and have invariably sealed their letters with their thumbs." Certainly his father did not impress him, though he admitted that the old gentleman improved with age. But he was devoted to his mother, a lady of French descent, whose delicate health was partly due to her husband's extraordinary behavior; for he had left her at the door of the church immediately after their marriage, gone straight to America, knocked about the world for several years, returned, consummated the union, and spent the rest of his life in "buying, altering, spoiling and then selling about nineteen different places in England." These rapid and

frequent changes of address were not favorable to healthy pregnancy, and though Mrs. Smith bore him four sons and a daughter, she did not live long to enjoy their society.

The Smiths were at Woodford in Essex on the third of June, 1771, when their second child, Sydney, was born. After a brief schooling at Southampton, he accompanied another brother to Winchester, where he was ill-fed, ill-treated, and thoroughly unhappy. He was, however, a brilliant scholar and eventually became captain of the school. The practical sense that distinguished him in later life was early developed. Being hungry, and noting a particularly fat turkey in the headmaster's yard, he made a catapult. The headmaster, seeing the instrument, complimented him on his ingenuity, but failed to put two and two together when the bird disappeared. From Winchester, Sydney went to New College, Oxford, where he obtained a fellowship of £100 a year and lived on it for the rest of his time at the university. He even paid his brother's school debts of £30 out of this meager income ("I did it with my heart's blood," he said many years later), and the fact that he seldom mentioned his Oxford days in later life proves that he was miserable there. Though he would have liked to follow his elder brother to the bar, he could not afford it, and on leaving Oxford he entered the Church.

In 1794 he was appointed to the curacy of Nether Avon on Salisbury Plain, where he endured three years of comparative solitude, the chief event of the place being the arrival once a week of the butcher's cart from Salisbury. "My preaching," he declared, "is like the voice of one crying in the wilderness." But he did his best for the inhabitants, establishing the first Sunday school in the locality; starting an industrial school to teach the girls knitting, sewing, and darning; and taking so much interest in the personal concerns of his widely scattered parishioners that eventually they became aware of a church in their midst and showed enough interest in him to gape through his sermons. "Nothing can equal the profound, the immeasurable, the awful dullness of this place," he wrote, "in which I lie, dead and buried, in hopes of a joyful resurrection in the year 1796." But the patron of his living, Michael Hicks-Beach, had taken a great fancy to him, and Sydney left Nether Avon for Edinburgh as tutor and companion to Beach's son, who had entered the university there.

They reached the city in June, 1798, and Sydney soon got to know some of the young intellectuals then struggling into fame—the critic Francis Jeffrey, the jurist Henry Brougham, the barrister John Murray, the poets Walter Scott and Thomas Campbell, and the politician-economist Francis Horner. Here he stayed for five years, studying medicine, preaching, taking pupils, making good jokes, and eating bad food. "Never shall I forget the happy days I passed there," he exclaimed, "amidst odious smells, barbarous sounds, bad suppers, excellent hearts, and most enlightened and cultivated understandings!" He felt that the Scots were deficient in a sense of humor: "It requires a surgical operation to get a joke well into a Scotch understanding." And he found them "so imbued with metaphysics that they even make love metaphysically." Some years later he wrote to Lady Holland, the hostess whose house became the social and intellectual center of the English Whigs: "I take the liberty to send you two brace of grouse—curious, because killed by a Scotch metaphysician; in other and better language, they are mere ideas, shot by other ideas, out of a pure intellectual notion, called a gun." He could never make head or tail of their theology: "It is in vain that I study the subject of the Scotch Church. I have heard it ten times over from Murray, and twenty times from Jeffrey, and I have not the smallest conception what it is about. I know it has something to do with oatmeal, but beyond that I am in utter darkness."

In June, 1800, he visited England in order to marry Catherine Pybus of Cheam, Surrey, who brought him a modest dowry, his own contribution to their fortune being "six small silver teaspoons, which, from much wear, had become the ghosts of their former selves." A little later Hicks-Beach sent him a present of £750. His marriage was an exceptionally happy one.

The friendship between Jeffrey, Brougham, Horner, and himself was epoch-making. Horner, he said, was "so extremely serious about the human race that I am forced to compose my face half a street off before I meet him." As for Jeffrey, soon to become a ruling critic of English letters, a little more modesty would have become him. Said Sydney: "I once heard him speak disrespectfully of the Equator." Brougham, like all famous reformers, was intensely egotistical. In fact, they were the right type of men to make a success of Sydney's great scheme.

On a stormy night in March, 1802, Sydney propounded his idea of a revolutionary periodical to Brougham and Jeffrey. The latter was full of doubts and fears, but Sydney laughed and argued him out of his timidity, and the *Edinburgh Review* was started. These three, with Horner, were the pioneers of a literary and political movement they could scarcely have foreseen. Though Sydney supervised the first number, Jeffrey eventually became the editor. For many years Sydney contributed to it, and his writings did more to popularize it than anything else. Toleration was his main theme, as it was the chief characteristic of the man, and there was hardly any form of tyranny and bigotry that he did not riddle with ridicule. The Game Laws, the slave trade, the Poor Laws, religious fanaticism, the state of Ireland, the persecution of the Catholics, the Court of Chancery, the barbarity of the Penal Laws, the cruelty to which chimney boys were subjected—there were few subjects upon which the light of his irony did not play, few forms of oppression that he did not expose. Though a Whig in politics, he was a humanist and a humorist before everything, which accounts for the fact that when his party came into power his services in the cause of progress were never fully recognized or rewarded. His realistic view of politicians scarcely improved his chances of preferment. "When a man is a fool," he remarked, "in England we only trust him with the immortal concerns of human beings." And he once referred to "the *rattery* and scoundrelism of public life."

Leaving Edinburgh in 1803, Sydney settled in London, took a small house in Doughty Street, became evening preacher to the Foundling Hospital at £50 a year, and soon officiated as morning preacher at a chapel in Mayfair. Later he delivered a course of lectures on moral philosophy at the Royal Institution. These met with enormous success and were the talk of fashionable London. He called them the greatest literary imposture of the age, and said he was heartily ashamed of his own fame. Nevertheless he thoroughly enjoyed his popularity, which enabled him to take a pleasant house in Orchard Street, to give suppers to his friends, and to be received on equal terms by the wits of Holland House. He was soon intimate with Richard Brinsley Sheridan, Charles James Fox, Lord Holland, the society versifier Henry Luttrell, the poets Samuel Rogers and Thomas Moore, and the philosopher James Mackintosh; he was invited everywhere and became a leader of conversation. He was a tall man of ample proportions, with a merry eye in a jovial face. "I certainly am the best-looking man concerned with the *Review*," he told Jeffrey, "and this Murray has been heard to say behind my back." He greatly admired good manners, especially in women: "I was much struck with the politeness of Miss Markham. . . . In carving a partridge, I splashed her with gravy from head to foot; and though I saw three distinct brown rills of animal juice trickling down her cheek, she had the complaisance to swear that not a drop had reached her! Such circumstances are the triumphs of civilized life." And he was at one with Jeffrey on feminine beauty: "The information of very plain women is so inconsiderable, that I agree with you in setting no very great store by it. . . . Where I have seen fine eyes, a beautiful complexion, grace and symmetry in women, I have generally thought them amazingly well-informed and extremely philosophical. In contrary instances, seldom or never. Is there any accounting for this?" Occasionally he went into the country, but he did not like it: "I am undergoing that species of hybernation, or suspended existence, called a pleasant fortnight in the country. I behave myself quietly and decently, as becomes a corpse, and hope to regain the rational and immortal part of my composition about the 20th of this month."

During this period he wrote and published anonymously *Peter Plymley's Letters*, which did more than any single thing to bring about the emancipation of the Catholics. In 1806 Lord Holland managed to obtain for him the living of Foston-le-Clay in Yorkshire. But in those days the clergy were not compelled to reside in their parishes, and it was not until after the passing of the Residence Act that Sydney Smith decided to tear himself away from London and, since there was no house fit for occupation in Foston, transport his family to Heslington, some miles from his parish. Most of the country clergy of that time were more interested in sport than religion, and Sydney informed Lady Holland that "if anything ever endangers the Church, it will be the strong propensity to shooting for which the clergy are remarkable. Ten thousand good shots dispersed over the country do more harm to the cause of religion than the arguments of Voltaire and Rousseau." He settled down to his duties with a will and soon became popular with the countryfolk. "Instead of being unamused by trifles," he declared, "I am, as I well knew I should be, amused by them a great deal too much; I feel an ungovernable interest about my horses, or my pigs, or my plants; I am forced, and always was forced, to task myself up into an interest for any higher objects." When Lady Holland wondered how such a social person as he could endure a life among rustics and turnips, he replied: "As long as I can possibly avoid it, I will never be unhappy. If, with a pleasant wife, three children, a good house and farm, many books, and many friends who wish me well, I cannot be happy, I am a very silly, foolish fellow, and what becomes of me is of very little consequence." Still, he did not minimize the dullness. Speaking of someone who wished to visit him, he delivered a necessary warning: "Nothing can exceed the dullness of this place," qualifying it with the comment "but he has been accustomed to live alone with his grandmother, which, though a highly moral life, is not a very amusing one."

He studied baking, brewing, poultry-fattening, churning, and suchlike things; he observed that "all animals have a passion for scratching their backbones," and to save his gates and hedges from destruction he placed in every field a sharp-edged pole for that purpose; he tried to economize on candles by burning the fat of his sheep; he improved grates and went into the subject of smoking chimneys; he instituted allotments for the poor, and became the doctor of the parish. Though it was his firm opinion that every person of sense hates exercise, he was never idle, and seldom sat down except to eat or to write letters or articles for the *Edinburgh Review*. The breeding of sheep absorbed his attention for a while, and he came to the conclusion that certain kinds of sheep were only called Scotch to signify ill-fed, "as one says Roman, to signify *brave*."

At length he determined to build a parsonage at Foston. "I live trowel in hand," he said. He must indeed have been extremely busy; for, while building his house (without an architect), he was educating his eldest son, farming his lands (with the assistance of a telescope and a speaking trumpet, through which, to save time, he shouted orders to the laborers), attending his wife in a confinement, physicking the parish, doing the work of a justice of the peace, and not neglecting his duties as a clergyman. In the midst of these labors he found time to dine occasionally with newly made friends in the neighborhood of York, and sometimes managed to horrify the more serious among them. At one dinner he suddenly declared that, though he was not generally considered an illiberal man, yet he had to confess one little weakness, one secret wish—he would like to roast a Quaker.

"Good heavens, Mr. Smith!" cried another guest in dismay, "Roast a Quaker?!"

"Yes, sir," replied Sydney with the utmost gravity, "roast a Quaker!"

"But do you not consider the terrible torture?"

"Yes, sir, I have considered everything. It may be wrong, as you say; the Quaker would undoubtedly suffer acutely; but everyone has his tastes, and mine would be to roast a Quaker. *One* would satisfy me, only one. I hope you will pardon my weakness, but it is one of those peculiarities I have striven against in vain."

The gentleman was so upset that Sydney was at last forced to explain that he had only meant it as a joke.

As a clergyman his practice was more acceptable to his parishioners than his preaching. In the pulpit he was too much of a Christian to be thought orthodox; he preached toleration for all creeds and made his own as jolly and comfortable as possible. He described some friends as having become "a little too Methodistical. I endeavour in vain to give them more cheerful ideas of religion; to teach them that God is not a jealous, childish, merciless tyrant; that he is best served by a regular tenour of good actions—not by bad singing, ill-composed prayers, and eternal apprehensions. But the luxury of false religion is to be unhappy." He had a great admiration for Elizabeth Fry, the famous prison reformer, and accounted for her unpopularity with the clergy in this manner: "Examples of living, active virtue disturb our repose and give birth to distressing comparisons: we long to burn her alive."

He disliked the mortification of the flesh. "Let me warn you against the melancholy effects of temperance," he said to a friend, "depend upon it, the wretchedness of human life is only to be encountered upon the basis of meat and wine." This good advice took root, and a little later he was able to congratulate the friend on his improved health as a result of making "very laudable resolutions of intemperance." Sydney's opinion of his professional brethren may be gathered from the postscript to one of his letters: "You have met, I hear, with an agreeable clergyman: the existence of such a being has been hitherto denied by the naturalists; measure him, and put down on paper what he eats." He had an especial objection to the hierarchy: "If you know that the Bishops are to be massacred, write by return of post." One of his remarks explains why the upper clergy were a little uneasy with him: "I must believe in the Apostolic Succession, there being no other way of accounting for the descent of the Bishop of Exeter from Judas Iscariot." Their nervousness would not have been dispelled by his comment on Dean Milman's *History of Christianity Under the Empire:* "No man should write on such subjects unless he is prepared to go the whole *lamb*." On the other hand, he would stand up for the Church when it was attacked by a layman. During a heated argument with a country squire, his opponent became abusive. "If I had a son who was an idiot, by Jove, I'd make him a parson!" bawled the squire. "Very probably," was Sydney's gentle reply, "but I see that your father was of a different mind."

He never complained of his lot, though he longed for London. His constitutional gaiety helped him over all the difficulties of life, and he could honestly say: "I thank God, who has made me poor, that he has made me merry." He boasted that he lived with doors and windows wide open, that anyone could know whatever they wanted to know about him in five minutes. His fondness for the good things of life never left him. Excusing himself for not having replied to a letter, he remarked: "Lord Tankerville has sent me a whole buck; this necessarily takes up a good deal of my time." And he breathed forth this pious prayer: "May mankind continue to set forth a tenth of the earth's produce for the support of the clergy; inasmuch as it is known to draw a blessing on the other nine parts, and is wonderfully comfortable to all ranks and descriptions of persons." On another occasion he acknowledged a present in these terms: "What is real piety? What is true attachment to the Church? How are these fine feelings best evinced? The answer is plain: by sending strawberries to a clergyman. Many thanks." This sort of attitude could be a little disconcerting. Imploring him to attend a large party, the hostess used the expression: "We shall be on our knees to you if you come." His reply shocked her: "I'm glad to hear it. I like to see you in that attitude, as it brings me in several hundreds a year."

He was prodigal of good advice on every kind of matter. "Geranium-fed bacon is of a beautiful colour," he wrote to someone whose pigs had been raiding the flower garden, "but it takes so many plants to fatten one pig that such a system can never answer." He devised a novel method of preserving the crops: "A very wet harvest here; but I have saved all my corn by injecting large quantities of fermented liquors into the workmen, and making them work all night." His chief vexation was the severe recurrence of hay fever during the summer months. Warm weather never agreed with him. "I am, you know, of the family of Falstaff," he said, and though he was referring to his body, he could with some truth have said it of his mind. He was becoming more and more realistic in his personal attitude to world affairs as the years went by, and there was not a little of Falstaff's philosophy in his heartfelt cry to the prime minister's wife: "For God's sake, do not drag me into another war! I am worn down, and worn out, with crusading and defending Europe, and protecting mankind; I *must* think a little of myself. I am sorry for the Spaniards—I am sorry for the Greeks—I deplore the fate of the Jews—the people of the Sandwich Islands are groaning under the most detestable tyranny—Bagdad is oppressed—I do not like the present state of the Delta—Tibet is not comfortable. Am I to fight for all these people? The world is bursting with sin and sorrow. Am I to be champion of the Decalogue, and to be eternally raising fleets and armies to make all men good and happy? We have just done saving Europe, and I am afraid that the consequence will be that we shall cut each other's throats. No war, dear Lady Grey!—no eloquence; but apathy, selfishness, common sense, arithmetic!"

In 1825 he attended a meeting of the clergy of the diocese and spoke in favor of Catholic emancipation, finding himself in a minority of one. The next year he spent a short holiday in Paris, writing to his wife daily therefrom. One report ran: "I dined with Lord Holland. There was at table Barras, the ex-Director, in whose countenance I immediately discovered all the signs of blood and cruelty which distinguished his conduct. I found out, however, at the end of dinner, that it was not Barras, but M. de Barante, an historian and man of letters, who, I believe, has never killed anything greater than a flea." During the brief

Coalition Government of 1827 Sydney became a canon of Bristol Cathedral, celebrating the event with a sermon on toleration for Catholics before the mayor and Corporation, which so outraged that worthy body that "several of them could not keep the turtle on their stomachs." Shortly after his appointment he went for the first time to Court "with, horrible to relate, strings to my shoes instead of buckles—not from Jacobinism but ignorance. . . . I found to my surprise people looking down at my feet. At first I thought they had discovered the beauty of my legs, but at last the truth burst on me, and gathering my sacerdotal petticoats about me, like a lady conscious of thick ankles, I escaped further observation."

He managed to exchange the living of Foston for that of Combe Florey, a charming village near Taunton, and here he was soon at work beautifying the parsonage and learning, from watching the workmen, that "a straight line in Somersetshire is that which includes the greatest possible distance between the extreme points." In spite of the beauty of his surroundings, he could never feel enthusiastic about the country, which he described as "a kind of healthy grave." Gradually he settled down to the routine of parish work; and since he did not shoot or hunt, his one rural amusement was to dose his parishioners, though he left the cases of scarlet fever "to the professional and graduated homicides."

*The young Queen Victoria was often carried away by fits of laughter at the sayings of Sydney Smith, as related by her prime minister and riding companion Lord Melbourne.*

As he was now getting on in life he determined to behave "like a dignitary of the Church, by confining myself to digestion . . . I am convinced digestion is the great secret of life, and that character, talent, virtues and qualities, are powerfully affected by beef, mutton, pie-crust, and rich soups." He ceased to contribute to the *Edinburgh Review* because he felt he had done enough in that way. "I love liberty, but hope it can be so managed that I shall have soft beds, good dinners, fine linen, etc., for the rest of my life. I am too old to fight or to suffer." He had not yet given up all hope of promotion and believed Lord Grey, if he became prime minister, might do something for him, "but the upper parsons live vindictively, and evince their aversion to a Whig ministry by an improved health. The Bishop of Ely has the rancor to recover after three paralytic strokes, and the Dean of Lichfield to be vigorous at eighty-two—and yet these are men who are called Christians." However, the prospect of a witty bishop was too much for sovereign or ministers of either party, and before he was seventy Sydney himself had ceased to wish for promotion, unaffectedly delighted though he was when his early companions in the struggle for reform, Jeffrey, Brougham, Murray, were raised to the peerage.

He received visits from all his old friends at Combe Florey. His fellow wit at Holland House, Luttrell, came and was very agreeable, "but spoke too lightly, I thought, of veal soup. I took him aside, and reasoned the matter with him, but in vain. To speak the truth, Luttrell is not steady in his judgments on dishes." Further, his ignorance on certain matters of importance was profound: "Luttrell, before I taught him better, imagined that muffins grew!" Another visitor of note who had written a book on the danger of increasing the population was received with care: "Philosopher Malthus came here last week. I got an agreeable party for him of unmarried people. There was only one lady who had had a child; but he is a good-natured man, and, if there are no appearances of approaching fertility, is civil to every lady."

When the Whigs returned to power in 1831 Lord Grey made Sydney a canon of St. Paul's Cathedral, London. "I asked for nothing—never did anything shabby to procure preferment," said he, "—these are pleasing recollections." But shortly after the appointment was announced he did something that made his name a household word throughout the land. Speaking at Taunton, he compared the attitude of the House of Lords to the Reform Bill with that of Dame Partington to the Atlantic Ocean during a storm at Sidmouth, in words that were repeated up and down the country and illustrated in prints that were displayed in almost every shop window:

In the midst of this sublime and terrible storm, Dame Partington, who lived on the beach, was seen at the door of her house with mop and pattens, trundling her mop, squeezing out the sea-water, and vigorously pushing away the Atlantic Ocean. The Atlantic

CONTINUED ON PAGE 124

MORRIS ENGEL

# RUTH ORKIN'S NEW YORK

New York City is the most hackneyed photographic subject in America. It has been shot from every angle, at every hour, by everyone from the tourist with his Brownie to the professional festooned with equipment. One might think that everything about it had been said. But the glimmering cityscapes presented in gravure on the following eight pages prove that an accomplished photographer can still make the city his own, projecting a vision of it as personal as a painter's.

These photographs are the work of Ruth Orkin, who is seen above in the window of her fifteenth-floor apartment from which she shot them all. The great oasis of Central Park lay spread out before her; towers rose beyond to the south and east. She wanted to see how much variety she could get from one position with limited equipment as the city's face changed with times of day and seasons. As a result, she says, "I felt that nature was designing the pictures for me, instead of my trying to manipulate it. All I had to decide was when to shoot." One of the most arresting designs is the final picture in this portfolio, where a bolt of lightning so startled Miss Orkin that she jiggled the camera slightly.

Ruth Orkin is a new name as a landscape photographer. She is far better known for her candid still photographs of people—revealing genre sequences out of everyday life, such as the three little card players at the left—and for the motion pictures she has made with her husband, Morris Engel.

All of these—movies, stills, and landscapes—have one thing in common: they are generally about New York. In the movies and still photographs it is the city's people that matter. Here, in these landscapes, she has looked squarely at the panorama of New York itself. What she saw, and captured during her many hours at the window, is the splintered skyline, the moody weather, the quicksilver light of the vast, improbable city.

# WHEN FORGERY BECOMES A FINE ART

*By* GILBERT HIGHET

It is a delicate and ambiguous phrase, "artistic forgeries." It ought to mean "spurious imitations of works of art." But it can also signify "fakes which in themselves are works of art." They belong to the history of polite crime, these graceful counterfeits. No violence attended their birth; their maturity was welcomed, not with cries of alarm, but with murmurs of admiration; and even when their discovery approached, it came in discreet silence, broken only by the indrawn breath of astonishment, a gasp just loud enough to conceal the victim's low groan and the spectator's stifled guffaw.

One of the loveliest things in the Louvre is not shown today to the public. You see it here on the page following. It is a sumptuous golden headdress, something between a crown and a helmet, handsomely embossed with figures of animals wild and tame, circles of leaves and branches and flowers and fruit, fine geometrical patterns, and a broad central zone showing men and women, horses and trees, gracefully arranged and strongly designed. It bears a Greek inscription saying that it was presented by the remote Greek city of Olbia (in what is now the Ukraine) to the Scythian chief Saitaphernes at a time corresponding to our third century B.C. The Louvre bought it for a good stout price in 1896. To anyone except a highly skilled expert, it would appear to be both genuine and enjoyable. But it is a fake. It was made in a workshop in Odessa, a few years before it was sold to the Louvre. Its craftsman, Israel Rouchomovsky, turned up in Paris in 1903, and identified his work. He had made the tiara convincing by using ancient designs taken from Greek and Roman cups and dishes and friezes; and, with an innate sense of proportion, he had even made it beautiful in a lavish, semibarbaric way. It was a fraud, yes, but it was an artistic forgery.

Cheap and easy fakes flood the market nowadays. The men who make them are not even interested in art. Nor are those who buy them. The fakers want to make money easily and rapidly. The purchasers want a rarity which is resalable and is guaranteed by its signature ("M. UTRILLO V." in a shaky, childish script) or its technique (everyone knows Renoir was partially paralyzed toward the end). As the satirist Samuel Butler put it, "doubtless the pleasure is as great of being cheated, as to cheat."

Think therefore of the delight experienced on both sides of a transaction that took place just before the Second World War. A South American millionaire, returning home from Europe, bought a Titian from a noble Italian family through a shrewd and tactful dealer. Admittedly, the papers of justification were not very copious, but after all, the painting had been four hundred years in the same family! The payment was made; the commission was taken. Remained the problem: how to get the picture out of Italy, in the face of stringent laws controlling the export of masterpieces from the homeland. Also, the purchaser did not quite trust the dealer, who might just conceivably notify the Italian authorities about a Titian which was being exported without authority, and then pocket the reward. So, after careful thought, the South American went to a trustworthy Roman artist, who painted a portrait of Mussolini over the Titian. Arriving in Buenos Aires, he took the picture to a restorer. Without difficulty, the restorer removed the portrait of Mussolini, and disclosed Titian's *Judgment of Cercyon*. However, he noticed that some of the painting in the *Judgment of Cercyon* was a bit weak. In order to strengthen it and prepare it for reinforcement, he went down further, scraped more of the paint away, and in due course disclosed, below the Titian, another portrait of Mussolini.

Not artistic. Cynically amusing, but devoid of real feeling. In most countries of the civilized world, you can buy a cheaply constructed and easily recognizable fake, with a famous name attached to it, but with no trace of real, or even imitative, distinction.

But these things are produced by hacks and intended for dupes. They are not truly artistic forgeries, such as the Tiara of Saitaphernes. To produce a fraud like that, one must be an expert, a lover of art, almost a creator. To detect it, one must be an expert, a lover of art, almost a complete cynic. One of the strangest cases of such forgery, detected by two young men using remarkable acumen and industry, caused great alarm and despondency in the quiet and thoughtful little world of rare-book collectors; it blasted several important reputations, depreciated the values of certain well-established rarities, and gave a pure pleasure to

105

Magnificent in appearance and complete with an ancient inscription, the gold tiara of
Saitaphernes was bought by the Louvre as a third-century B.C. prize. Yet it is a modern fake.

all those who admired the methods of Sherlock Holmes. "Detection," said that master of investigation, "is, or ought to be, an exact science, and should be treated in the same cold and unemotional manner."

One of the greatest prizes for any collector of rare books is the first edition of a work by a distinguished author. The first edition, even in its mistakes and eccentricities, shows the original intention of the writer; it may be far more rare than later editions; and, next to the actual manuscript, it has the romantic charm of any original creation.

Now, sometimes authors who are unusually ambitious or unusually scrupulous will have small private editions of their books printed, either so that they may check the typography, or so that they may distribute them to their friends before the first edition is made up for sale to the general public. A copy of such a private edition (sometimes called a "pre-first" edition) is bound to be very uncommon, very special, and very intimately connected with the author's own personality and artistic standards: therefore it is always a most valuable find for a book collector.

That excellent poet Robert Browning married a fairly good poet, Elizabeth Barrett. One of the best things she ever wrote was a collection of sonnets dealing with the growth of her love for him—graceful pieces on a delicate subject. When she issued them to the world, they were disguised as translations from another language: she called them *Sonnets from the Portuguese*. They came out in 1850.

But there are in existence several dozen copies of those same sonnets which seem to be three years earlier. They claim, on their title page, to be *Sonnets* by E. B. B., printed at Reading in 1847 for private circulation only. Their existence was accounted for by a story told by Edmund Gosse, most eminent of English critics. Soon after she had written the sonnets and shown them to her delighted husband, Mrs. Browning had sent the manuscript to her friend Mary Mitford; and Mary Mitford had produced a few copies on a small private printing press in Reading, to be given only to the most intimate friends of the Brownings. Presumably Miss Mitford kept a few copies of her special printing job, which came onto the market after her death. They were beautiful copies, too, in "mint condition," apparently never even read: no wonder people would pay over a thousand dollars for a single example.

Several other books like this appeared in the rare-book auctions during the first years of this century—scarce first editions, or pre-first editions, of essays and poems by Tennyson, by Ruskin, by Arnold, by Swinburne. A Chicago millionaire named John Henry Wrenn (who left all his rare books to the University of Texas) had a tremendous collection of about fifty of these very rare items. The Widener Library in Harvard had about twenty-five; the British Museum dug into the pocket of the British taxpayer for about thirty. Other collectors had only two or three; but they were all believed to be genuine treasures.

In 1934 two young men produced a very suave and objective little book which most reviewers would be tempted to dismiss as a dull piece of technical research because of its scrupulously modest title: *An Enquiry into the Nature of Certain Nineteenth Century Pamphlets*, by John Carter and Graham Pollard. But in fact it was a sensational little book. It showed conclusively that the pre-first edition of Elizabeth Barrett Browning's love sonnets was a forgery—an artistic forgery, because it was a little book of pleasing appearance, and had imposed on many of the leading specialists in a realm where fakes are both multifarious and ingenious. It was a forgery, and so were about fifty other books of the same type, all, until then, classified as valuable rarities.

Until 1932 this had never been suspected by more than a few men, and had certainly never been said out loud. However, Carter and Pollard, working over the master edition of John Ruskin's works, noticed that one of the editors declared (in a small-type footnote) that certain so-called first printings of Ruskin's books were forgeries, because their text resembled that of comparatively late versions, and not that of the known early copies. They also knew that certain reliable dealers would not touch these particular "first editions." They thought that there must be something fishy about the Ruskins and about similar rarities. So they began to apply scientific tests.*

They took the rare pre-first edition of Elizabeth Browning's sonnets and asked an analytical chemist to examine the paper on which it was printed. He found that it was made of chemically treated wood pulp. Chemical treatment for wood pulp was not introduced into the papermaking industry until the early 1880's. But the Browning pamphlet was dated 1847. Furthermore, Carter and Pollard found that ten of the rare editions which boasted, on their title pages, of having been published before 1861 were printed on paper containing esparto grass. Esparto grass was not used in papermaking until 1861.

Then the two detectives examined the type with which the Browning sonnets were printed. It had several notable characteristics. One of them was that the letters had no kerns. A kern is that part of a letter which projects beyond its ordinary rectangular shape: for instance, the curling tail of the letter *j* usually projects, and so does the curling forelock of the letter *f*. The type of the 1847 Browning sonnets and of some other rare pamphlets had no kerns. But the history of printing shows that alphabets without kerns were not introduced anywhere in the world until 1883 or so.

Next, Carter and Pollard discovered the printing firm that had possessed the type font with the kernless letters and other peculiarities in it, the firm of Richard Clay & Sons Ltd. They asked the firm whether it had ever printed the

*All this part of the detective process is admirably described by Richard D. Altick in a fascinating book called *The Scholar Adventurers*, published by Macmillan in 1950, to which I am deeply indebted.

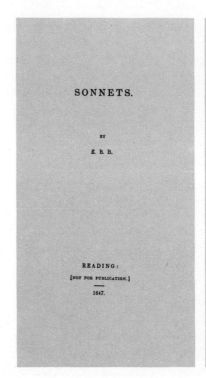

SONNETS.

BY

E. B. B.

READING:

[NOT FOR PUBLICATION.]

———

1847.

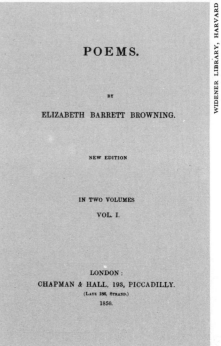

POEMS.

BY

ELIZABETH BARRETT BROWNING.

NEW EDITION

IN TWO VOLUMES

VOL. I.

LONDON:

CHAPMAN & HALL, 193, PICCADILLY.

(LATE 186, STRAND.)

1850.

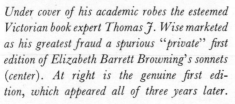

*Under cover of his academic robes the esteemed Victorian book expert Thomas J. Wise marketed as his greatest fraud a spurious "private" first edition of Elizabeth Barrett Browning's sonnets (center). At right is the genuine first edition, which appeared all of three years later.*

*Sonnets* by E. B. B. for a private customer. The firm replied that all its records for the period before 1911 (during which these forgeries entered the market) had been destroyed; so this part of the investigation ended abruptly, if suspiciously.

Now the investigators worked on another series of clues, some of which they had already collected. They set out to reconstruct the personality of the man who had made these artistic forgeries and to discover how he had fed them into the sensitive and suspicious rare-book market. Very few people had written authoritatively about these rare early editions. Some were obviously innocents, who appeared to have been intermediaries, passive assistants used to disseminate carefully planted false information. But one or two others were much more suspicious. Then Carter and Pollard traced the dealer who had actually sent many scores of these rarities to auctions. He was a London bookseller, and he willingly showed them his accounts. All his hundreds of copies had been obtained from the same man. Who was that one man? Now they had his name; but it was almost incredible. The one man who had unloaded the forgeries on the bookseller and had written articles in the specialist magazines explaining their origin and had maintained a large account with Richard Clay & Sons, this was one of the most distinguished book specialists in the whole world, one of the few supreme experts whose word alone could

settle a dispute about primacy or originality, a man rich and knowledgeable and respected. He was then seventy-four years of age, and his character and his experience had never been emphatically questioned. His name was Thomas J. Wise.

Young Pollard called on him. Wise professed complete astonishment when he was told what the investigators had discovered. It was all a woeful mistake, he said; he would review his memory and write them an account of the true facts. But, after months of waiting, no letter arrived. And so, nearly a year later, in July, 1934, the two bibliographers issued their book, which, with feline tact, was printed by Richard Clay & Sons. It did not accuse Thomas Wise of making the forgeries. It did show conclusively that most of this particular class of "first editions" were forgeries; and that if Wise had not forged them, he must have known the forger or else have been such a dullard that he had not seen through them. His reputation was gone. Either Wise was stupid, or Wise was dishonest. It was like accusing an eminent doctor either of killing his patients by poison, or of signing bogus death certificates, or of bungling his treatments so badly that when his patients died he could not recognize their terminal ailments. Wise wrote letters to the papers protesting in general terms against the implications of *An Enquiry into the Nature of Certain Nineteenth Century Pamphlets*, but very few people were convinced. In 1937 he died, unvindicated. Since his death conclusive evidence of his guilt has appeared in his own handwriting.*

When a complex and difficult crime such as forgery is committed, the motives for it lie fairly deep in the character of the forger. Even the simplest type of counterfeiting, copying a name on a check or imitating a bank note, needs a peculiar type of mind to execute it. But a forgery carried out with such taste and expertness that it is almost a work of art in itself cannot have been the outcome of a merely casual impulse: it must have been long planned, as a satisfaction for certain desires which exerted pressure on the criminal for a long time. No single urge is a sufficient motive. Many different passions must converge on a brilliant mind before it abandons its normal course, turns deliberately away, and takes a direction which it knows to be wrong.

The line between deliberate forgery and intelligent imitation is difficult to draw, and perhaps the first thing that edged Thomas Wise off the rails was his ability to make and to sell acknowledged facsimiles of rare books. These were not forgeries. They were artistic reproductions. There is a famous story about two brothers who lived in Florence many years ago, painting acknowledged copies of the Old Masters. They made a good living, they saved their money, and at last they took off for New York to see an uncle. They were transported with delight when they walked along the streets where art shops cluster like bees at the swarming season. The windows were full of original Italian masterpieces; and the brothers kept recognizing their own work, here labeled Veronese, there Bellini, here Lotto, and there Carracci.

In the long history of faked painting, there is one nonpareil: the Dutchman Hans van Meegeren. In 1937 or so he sold one of his own paintings to a museum in Rotterdam as a previously unknown religious work by that superb artist Jan Vermeer. The picture seemed to be moving, and suave, and delicate—all that an early Vermeer should be. It combined the thoughtful repose of Vermeer's best style with a certain warmth that might have been derived from Caravaggio—and Vermeer was known to have admired Caravaggio. But the thing had been painted with the deliberate intention of deceiving, by Hans van Meegeren.

Van Meegeren had worked hard to become famous as an original painter. His mind was vulgar, and he had no original sense of design: he had no success. But now, when his forged picture was accepted, he had become the creator of a masterpiece—even though the masterpiece was credited to a dead man. He could enjoy the two emotions of delight and disdain: delight in his own aesthetic sensibility, disdain for the foolish connoisseurs who had accepted a fake Vermeer as a real one; delight in the fact that he had made a large amount of money from the sale; disdain for the public that somehow had failed to recognize his genius unless in disguise; and supreme delight in the power of his own

*Details in John Carter's *Books and Book-Collectors* (World, 1957)

intellect and the intricacy of his stratagems. (He had taken enormous pains to reproduce the precise chemical composition of paint and canvas, the exact phenomena of aging—down to microscopic details—which would be exhibited in the twentieth century by a canvas that had been painted three hundred years earlier.) From this first success, Van Meegeren went on to forge and sell a good number of bogus Vermeers—some of them to shrewd Dutch collectors, some to that outstanding connoisseur Marshal Hermann Goering. But, such is the obstinacy, such is the pride of specialists that, when he finally confessed to his misdeeds, he had to paint an artistic forgery in person, under close surveillance, before the experts would admit that his other counterfeits were also no more than attractive traps.

Among the many motives that influence artistic forgers, one certainly is money. It takes much time to fake an apparently valuable work of art, much time and much effort. The forgers deal in works which are prized, and they grow to despise their customers who pay out good money for pieces which are doubtful. They come to think, therefore, that they will give the suckers anything to make them happy and meanwhile drain off for themselves some of that precious dirt which seems—by a strange inversion of the right order of things—to cling to suckers and not to artists. When Thomas Wise was executing some of his finest fakes, he was both building up one of the greatest private libraries in Britain and supporting a wife and child, on about £500 a year. Van Meegeren was a poor dauber, until he became rich by forging ahead.

There is another motive, more recondite. Van Meegeren was not only an unsuccessful painter; he was a dull and boring painter. Yet, if we look both at his own acknowledged works and the forgeries he produced, we can see what he was trying to do. He was attempting to rise above himself, by making himself into the newest and latest pupil and successor of Vermeer. Van Meegeren had scarcely any real ideals. Vermeer had deeply felt and utterly sincere ideals: so Van Meegeren adopted them. And in order to copy Vermeer, he had to work with unusual restraint, sensitivity, and care.

But among their other motives, forgers have one which is particularly strong. This is to outwit the experts. The general public (God bless us every one, said Tiny Tim) are simple souls. The experts are proud, lofty, difficult, sceptical, bitter, filled with hatred and distrust for any novelty. To challenge such men is a powerful enterprise; and therefore some men will dedicate their lives to do so.

The ultimate motive of the artistic forger is the impulse that drives many revolutionaries. He hates the contemporary world and wishes to humiliate it. He is determined to divert the course of history, so as to make himself a firm, secure place in the past, and to gain the prestige that has been denied to him by his own generation, the crude and insensitive present.

# SHOPPING WITH KAFKA

*By* JOHN KEATS

The modern supermarket rises from a level asphalt sea; its doors swing magically open as you approach, and a soft music plays within. It is a kind of air-conditioned, antiseptic, neon-lit fair—the burgeoning market place of the present and one clear indication of what our future may become: a spacious, odorless, dehumanized future, glittering with plenty of everything and the best of nothing.

This is no leisurely temple of bountiful Ceres. The supermarket is a sterile machine conceived by the kind of military mind that imagines beauty in terms of empty spaces, right angles, neatness, and obedience. Here are the commanding signs: "Frozen Foods—Section 36." Here is the disembodied voice of the loudspeaker that cannot be turned off. Here is efficiency—the maddening efficiency of the cans of identical soups that neatly flow from the gravity-feed shelves. Here is the totalitarian equality of the standard brand. It is impossible to enter a supermarket without being aware that you are in the thrall of an immense, anonymous corporate entity, infinitely cold and remote. You will not be able to select the ingredients of a meal—you'll take what you are offered. If you object, the store manager will put you in your place, for he is a *Gauleiter*. He and his underlings speak with the dispassionate accents of insect bureaucracy.

For example, let us say that you badly need one onion;

only one. There is no bin of onions. There are only piles of five-pound plastic bags of onions. You ask the white-uniformed stock clerk (if, indeed, you can find a clerk who does not rapidly walk away as you approach) about the possibility of purchasing one onion today.

"We sell 'em by the bag," he says, and turns, and goes.

As with onions, so with meats. You inspect the frosted sepulchers in which the meats are laid. Steak, as advertised, is unbelievably 85 cents a pound—but it is not U.S. Choice, much less U.S. Prime. It is Commercial grade, impervious to the doughtiest molar. The Choice costs more, but all steaks, of whatever grade, are sealed in those familiar fingernail-proof plastic packages, and you could slide any of them under your door.

You decide against the steaks. Nor do you wish to buy a transparent bag containing three pounds of grayish-pink hamburger for one dollar. You briefly consider bacon, then remember that supermarket bacon is so wrapped that it appears red and lean—but when you open the package at home, you discover that only the top eighth of an inch of each slice is meat and all the rest is pure lard. There *is*, however, a buzzer reserved for eccentrics who will not accept what they see, and you push it, the incarnation of eternal hope. After an indecent interval, a window opens behind the counter, and you learn what the American labor movement has become.

"Do you have Choice rib roasts?" you ask. "Three ribs, about eight pounds?"

"I won't be cutting meat until five o'clock," the union butcher says.

With that, the window slams shut, and you are left alone to push your tiny tumbrel through a market place that, strangely, does not smell of food. You move vaguely down the impersonal aisles, dimly aware of the soap that makes dishwashing hilarious, listening (for you cannot entirely close your ears) to Perry Como.

You remember a delicacy that Mr. Glotz used to sell, before Mr. Glotz was pushed out of his crowded, somewhat dirty corner grocery by the advent of the supermarket. You do not find it on the abstract shelves, and you put in a request, through channels, to speak with the *Gauleiter*. He appears—a waxy icicle. With equal willingness, devotion, and efficiency, he could manage another branch of the same, or any other, supermarket chain, no matter whether in Denver, Berlin, Philadelphia, or Omsk.

"We don't carry it," he says.

"Could you please get it for me if I put in an order?" you ask.

"No," he explains.

Wearily, you make what compromises you must, and join the line of pushers of identical carts at the checking-out counters, and after you have paid the price, the magical doors burst open with impersonal enthusiasm to permit you to leave.

Next customer!

It is usually said in defense of supermarkets that they offer greater variety than the old corner stores, that by serving yourself you reduce your shopping time, and that they enable more people to buy more food at lower prices.

But many supermarkets offer only their own brands. While there may be variety of foods, there is little choice of brand. Also, by virtue of their sheer size, such supermarkets seem to offer a greater variety of foods than actually exists, because once inside, you discover the store merely has many shelves full of the same thing.

As for convenience, the supermarket may be simply a larger version of the neighborhood store, in that no time is saved. That is, shoppers first spend uncounted hours hunting among the desert aisles, much as ants fitfully negotiate a maze. Then, having shopped, they wait in line to leave, and the length of the line might exactly equal the sum of the customers seen in the neighborhood grocery at any one time.

Finally, the notion that supermarkets provide more people with cheaper food is most often a snare and always a delusion. The giant savings that s-t-r-e-t-c-h your dollars are usually discovered in the area devoted to the sale, today, of the bakery stuffs that were not sold yesterday. Or, they are piled beneath the banners reading "Apple Jelly Festival! Stock up NOW on our economy-size jars of Mother Bloor's jelly! Six GIANT jars for 99¢!" Let us say you obediently stock up—as though you were preparing to operate a hotel, or withstand a siege. The first taste of this pectin, "with genuine U.S. Certified artificial color added," assures you there is nothing festive about it. Indeed, you are immediately finished with Mother Bloor's jelly for all time. Too late, you understand the reason for the sale.

Of course, there is nothing intrinsically wrong with a store that offers plenty of everything, if, indeed, it does. Nor is standardization necessarily evil in itself, nor can one quarrel with the concept of low prices for low quality. Nor is much wrong with neatness, except that humanity also requires an occasional display of that sweet disorder that enchanted the Cavalier poet. Indeed, there is nothing wrong with monopoly, per se, as Mr. Justice Holmes pointed out. Wherefore, let us not too loudly sweep the strings for poor Mr. Glotz with his sawdust floors and the flies on his peaches.

Still, we might be saved from today's supermarkets—and they for us—if someone would put Mr.

Glotz and his familiar clerks and butchers into that plate-glass and chromium food-dispensing machine in the shopping center. Mr. Glotz would first take the fruits out of their transparencies to permit the jolly odors of good things to return to the market place. His clerks would say important little nothings, such as "sir," and "ma'am," and "may I help you?" and "let me get it for you," and "thank you."

In a word, humanity would return to our shopping if Mr. Glotz *et cie.* were to replace the faceless automatons who currently mind the supermarket without interest in you, in themselves, or in their jobs. It would cost the supermarket nothing to exchange one staff for the other, and if it employed Mr. Glotz, perhaps at least some warmth would begin to fill the cold, neat spaces among the antiseptic aisles with their burden of sanitized,

vacuum-packed, Saf-Tee-Sealed foodstuffs which are not only warranted to be untouched by human hands, but which too often prove to be as impersonally odorless and tasteless as the store itself.

As matters stand, Mr. Glotz has been washed aside by the wave of the future, and the supermarket represents one more manifestation of giantism—the kind of giantism that helps to form the mass man, further reducing the possibility of one man privately meeting another face to face in the ordinary commerce of life. Just as we have giant school systems remote from public control, just as we have unions remote from the members' participation, just as we have businesses remote from even the nominal control of stockholders, just as we have government over which most people believe they have no control, so we have these giant stores which also tend to become totalitarian bureaucracies. All produce the modern version of the eternal human tragedy; replacing the classical Fates, our giantisms become the relentless forces which no man, no matter what his efforts, can hope to control. The unbearable irony in our modern tragedy, however, is that these uncontrollable giantisms are all man-made.

Unless Mr. Glotz—which is to say, humanity—is somehow miraculously returned to us, the supermarket will increasingly resemble a microcosm of the corporate state. Indeed, the resemblance is already far more than superficial, which is not surprising when we reflect that the supermarket, like any totalitarian world, is founded on an infinite lie. In the supermarket's case, the lie is "self-service." The fact is that supermarkets have so taken the personal relationship out of marketing that you can neither satisfy yourself nor obtain any service. And so we move like zombies through our neon and plate-glass nightmare, mindlessly —endlessly—shopping with the ghost of Franz Kafka.

---

*John Keats is the author of* The Crack in the Picture Window, The Insolent Chariots, *and other social studies.*

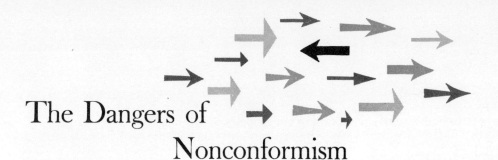

# The Dangers of Nonconformism

*Morris Freedman, a nonconforming nonconformist who teaches at the University of New Mexico, contributed to the Winter 1958-59 issue of* The American Scholar *an article under the above title, from which excerpts are here presented by permission of the publisher, the United Chapters of Phi Beta Kappa.*

Not long ago I heard one of this country's professional intellectuals—a former university president, a present foundation president—address a university gathering of several hundred persons. The gentleman attacked the blight of conformism in the United States; he deplored the fact that men in gray flannel suits had become "interchangeable"; he lamented the loss of true individualism. What struck me while listening to his urbane talk was his own "interchangeable" appearance: neat, three-button blue suit, plain tie, precisely coiffured graying hair, erect carriage: the very model of a model executive, not only interchangeable with dozens of men in similar positions and in "gentlemen of distinction" ads, but ready to be played in the movies by a dozen or so actors—Walter Pidgeon, Cary Grant, Gregory Peck, Ray Milland. It struck me as somewhat odd, too, that several hundred persons should applaud in unison a speech urging nonconformity, and that during the question period one of the questions that did not "conform" with the speaker's views should be greeted with derision.

Of course one man's conformism may be another man's heresy. But what seems to have taken place in American intellectual life in recent years is the rising of just about any nonconformity to the status of respectable orthodoxy.

It has been well-established that nonconformists, instead of responding to the values of tabloid newspaper, subway car, or television advertisements, respond to a no less specific and no less rigid set, particularly those in the advertisements of *The New York Times*, *The New Yorker*, the *Saturday Review* and the like, or of the commercials of FM stations that broadcast classical music all day. Although the nonconformist may refuse with a shudder to engage in the barbaric practice of drinking instant coffee, he will no less eagerly sip *espresso*. If you can construct a stereotype of the man in the street, you can build an equally plausible one of the man out of the street.

It was not so long ago that a position taken by a Luce publication would have been instinctively opposed by large numbers of nonconformists; but *Life* in recent years has so well caught the importance of being fashionably nonconformist that it is now a leader in establishing accepted nonconformist thought, which, of course, some while ago spilled over from the highbrow crest onto the extensive middle-brow plateaus. On the matter of education, for example, *Life* and other media shaping mass nonconformist ideology have now laid down the party line, making it intellectually suicidal to suggest that possibly the educators have their own peculiar problems to solve before they can reshape their curricula to respond to the present pressures. On most campuses, I venture, a professor in liberal arts would be read out of the ranks if he said a good word about colleges of education, let alone about educational television, which combines two bogeys.

Let me catalogue from my own recent experience a number of other positions, attitudes, and habits of behavior and thought no nonconformist in good standing can hold these days. These are, of course, subject to rapid change, like fashions in ladies' dress. Also, I should say, it is not essential to reject *all* to remain a respectable nonconformist—only most of them.

It is impossible, then, for the nonconformist to say a good word about Dulles, Nixon, Lyndon Johnson, or (since Dwight MacDonald's critique in *Commentary*) James Gould Cozzens, or a bad one about Henry James, Adlai Stevenson, Lionel Trilling, or Freud; to express approval of any television show (except *Omnibus*, Ed Murrow, or Sid Caesar), or of any American movie (except the inexpensive and badly lighted ones, or the solemn westerns, like *High Noon*); to dislike any foreign films (except those imitating American ones); to believe that you can buy ready-made a good hi-fi set; to wear a non-Ivy-league suit or long hair if a man, or to wear or not wear a sack dress if a woman (I am not sure what feminine nonconformism calls for at the moment); to prefer American cars to European; to believe that there may be any justice in the official position on Oppenheimer; to defend Western diplomacy on any basis; to invite company to dinner without candles on the table and chamber music in the background; to criticize Arthur Miller or Tennessee Williams as playwrights or otherwise; to like Tchaikovsky or Irving Berlin, or to dislike Leonard Bernstein or Mozart; to express admiration for Marilyn Monroe or any other American movie star; to disparage Alec Guinness; and so on. . . .

There is no more self-righteously, high-mindedly closed a mind than that of a nonconformist. He will begin every conversation with some such gambit as "I know this isn't a popular position, but. . . ." He will insist that no one since Galileo or Joan of Arc has had as much courage as he. Challenge him, and he will dismiss you as a peasant not worth his attention. "If you don't know what's wrong with American culture," I heard one champion nonconformist say down his nose to someone who mildly demurred on the subject, "then there's no point even talking with you."

*By* MORRIS FREEDMAN

# The Rules of Fashion Cycles

CONTINUED FROM PAGE 66

to imagine that when people's tastes in architecture are bent on either simplicity or elaboration, they should adhere to the opposite of one or the other in their clothing. But the most telling consideration of all is that it appears to be the workings of the human memory rather than comparative durabilities of goods which determine the major fashion rhythm. After two generations have passed, few people will remember a once-popular but long-outmoded direction of style change. By that time, basic design features reminiscent of the old style can be reintroduced as if they were fresh and novel.

What is more, we find that the reactions in taste which follow the excesses of either extreme tend to be almost as sharp and drastic in architecture and furnishings as in dress. The only difference is that, naturally enough, it takes a longer time to translate these taste changes into action—which is to say production—where the household is concerned.

Only a century ago (really a relatively short span in an art where style changes can scarcely be measured in terms briefer than generations) John Ruskin declared: "Ornamentation is the principal part of architecture." That dictum sounds well-nigh incredible to those of us brought up in the ascendancy of Frank Lloyd Wright, Gropius, Le Corbusier, and their functionalist followers. Yet thus did the acknowledged mentor of the most edified taste of his day herald the late-Victorian gingerbread.

However, it was only forty years later, in 1892, that Louis Sullivan, the first American exponent of modernism, was writing that "ornament is mentally a luxury, not a necessary," and that "it would be greatly for our aesthetic good, if we should refrain entirely from the use of ornament for a period of years, in order that our thought might concentrate acutely upon the production of buildings well formed and comely in the nude."

Sullivan's comment is a highly subtle one, for, in addition to his implied analogy with the history of dress, he left the door open to the return to a sense of the need for ornament. Indeed, this sense is activating leading architects of today such as Eero Saarinen and Edward Stone; witness, for example, their resort to vivid colors, varied textures, and fanciful contrivance of structurally nonrequisite patterns.

In a recent series of interviews, I found an overwhelming consensus among art experts and industrial designers that the functional school is already meeting its Waterloo in the monotony it has imposed on urban building and even on interior decoration. Our architects have come just about as close to architectural nudity as is either possible or endurable. Thus:

¶ Construction features which at one time may have served the cause of utility—the use of greater areas of glass for improved lighting is the most conspicuous example—are tending to become exaggerated to the point of perverting function through destruction of privacy, removal of protection from the sun, and so on.

¶ The "sincere" demonstrations of what various structural features—girders, reinforced concrete, cantilevering—are capable of doing have been carried perilously close to mere displays of virtuosity and are made to assume shapes that are of no practical value whatsoever. Ornament, once officially legislated out of existence, has cropped out again in the form of extreme displays of the marvels of engineering.

So ingrained with us today is the notion that nothing can be new and modern unless it is also stark and shocking that it is hard to imagine any new style wave in housing not following the edicts of Gropius, Le Corbusier, and other "modernists." Yet that is just what is happening.

In his valuable book, *The Tastemakers*, Russell Lynes concludes with no hesitation that as far as domestic architecture is concerned, the flat-roofed, cubistic, and glass-walled house has been almost totally superseded by something quite different, which, for want of a better name, he calls the "ranch house." Indeed, it appears quite evident that Le Corbusier's modernistic concept, "the machine for living," though a few examples of it are still being built, is itself rapidly becoming outmoded.

The contemporary American house is the suburban house. The number of families who live in mid-city homes (outside of apartments) or who can afford a second house in the country is no longer significant. The tremendous change in living habits that has been wrought by the automobile and also by the demands that the great corporation places on the family breadwinner is as epochal in its own way as the change in the social structure that took place in eighteenth-century England.

What are the central tendencies of the contemporary suburban house? What have been its origins, and what is its future?

The fundamental feature appears to be "one-level living" (a feature sometimes more a matter of semblance than reality, for living space is frequently provided at basement level or in a partially concealed second story). This is accompanied by picture windows, a gently sloping, peaked roof, and rather muted reference to one or more of the styles of the architectural past—which the eclectic school of architects used to copy so literally in the 1920's—or, at times, a watered-down suggestion of functionalism. Houses of this type are already labeled "modern" by the practicing real-estate agent, who is prone to refer to something in the Le Corbusier spirit as "international."

113

The search for the antecedents of structures of this type has been accompanied by a good deal of guesswork. Lynes, for example, mentions the pre-World War I bungalow (favored because of its anticipation of the picture window and overhanging eaves), the California ranch house (although, in point of historical accuracy, the bunk house might be more apt), the Cape Cod cottage, the Swiss chalet, and the Spanish-American mission. He might as readily have included the log cabin.

To ask whether the contemporary house is descended from the bungalow, the ranch house, the cottage, or whatnot seems to be irrelevant. None of these would have entered the picture in the first place unless supported by deeper forces. It is more to the point, perhaps, to ask whether one-level living may be in part a response to the cult of comfort, a recognition of the disappearance of live-in servants, or an attempt to reproduce in the suburbs the arrangement of the city apartment in which most exurbanites once lived.

But if my view of fashion reactions is substantially correct, the most relevant, as well as the simplest explanation, is that the low, rambling effect was a logical direction for architects to take in groping for a style markedly different from the boxlike, many-peaked domiciles of grandfather's day. If so, it is only too apparent that while the big guns on the battlefield of architectural doctrine were booming forth their conflicting dogmas, the unconscious desires of the public for something meaningfully new and different but still not too out of kilter with traditional sentiments, were in a quieter but more profound way shaping the look of the future. Such a conclusion does seem confirmed by the historical record, which shows that over the past fifty or more years the rambling house has steadily increased in frequency, no matter what style the designer told himself and his client he was working in.

Are fresh reactions against the simplified rambler in the

*Verticality in the eighteenth century*

making? Prediction, of course, does not follow automatically from analysis, largely because fashion may desert any particular variation for another. For example, the public and its architects may decide to leave the dimensions of the house as they are and concentrate rather on the introduction of new building materials, new colors, and the like. We can only suggest that after more than a half-century the trends toward architectural nudity and toward lowness have nearly reached the end of the road.

As early as 1954, in fact, home-building journals were beginning to report that in certain of the most populous areas of the country the "split-level" house (defined as a dwelling "with at least three separate levels, two of which are located one above the other, and all of which are one-half level apart in elevation") was actually outselling ranch types four to one. This halfway, yet decisive, return to verticality and a more "impressive" look is precisely what this analysis would lead us to expect.

The history of furniture demonstrates most notably that the central current of stylistic development, no matter how sharp its twistings and turnings, will carry elements of past and present.

The greater part of the public (and this is equally true at all levels of prestige and income) is motivated just as surely by a sense of loyalty to traditional sentiment as it is by the desire for novelty or considerations of utility. Such loyalty is the backbone of cultural continuity, just as willingness to adopt new materials or mechanical advantages is the backbone of progress. These two driving interests will separate at times and at other times come together. Once again: "There is room for audacity in the framework of tradition."

Whereas clothing is worn out and discarded, corrupted by moths, or hidden away in attics, neither the rage of the wrecker nor natural catastrophe ever completely obliterates the antique furniture of bygone eras. Because of its mobility, it offers the antique collector his golden opportunity, so that when most people hear the word *antique*, they think only of furniture. Consequently, the American house has been more profoundly influenced by past standards of design through its furniture (whether in the form of authentic period pieces or reproductions) than in any other way. To nomadic Americans furniture has become the chief material means of symbolizing family continuity.

To refer to the stylistic significance of antiquities in a study of fashion reactions—reactions already defined as arising from the pursuit of novelty for its own sake—is far less paradoxical than may appear to be the case at first glance. A curio from the remote past is just as apt to be considered a novelty as a new gadget or an exotic rarity. Back in the 1920's, for example, the suddenly discovered charm of colonial furniture was as much a novelty to those who succumbed to it as was the scientific miracle of the radio or the mysterious fascination of mah-jongg.

The antique serves as the most effective reminder of the

*The cap of fashion in 1795*

the scale to the toaster, alarm clock, and waffle iron.

Everything had to have rounded edges; everything had to look compact, sleek, and as if it were capable of going somewhere fast. Armed with the principle of streamlining, and some rather self-conscious claims to aesthetic cultivation which the factory-bound designers of grandma's coal range or grandpa's buggy lacked, the latter-day industrial designer succeeded in establishing a specialized form of big business.

great style periods of the past. It appeals to the sentiments we associate with great traditions, especially if it dates from one of the pioneering eras (such as eighteenth-century England was in furniture) whose rich creativity in design entitles it to be called classical. But every generation, as it swings back and forth along the great rhythm between elaboration and simplicity, will exercise its own particular preferences among all the styles of the past and its own special ideas about how to express them. Some will prefer the simpler, some the more ornate. Some will want their antiques or their reproductions "neat," others will want to doctor them up. In short, there are fashions in antiques as in everything else.

The furniture stores have for several decades stocked, side by side, "traditional" pieces, consisting of more or less faithful reproductions, and "modern" pieces, consisting largely of furniture featuring metal materials or newly treated forms of wood such as plywood, along with functional shapes based on theories of anatomical suitability.

Closer examination, nevertheless, will show that increasingly this apparent distinction has become less meaningful. More and more, the so-called modern has become dominated by pieces which, though they often show a significant degree of originality, conform essentially to eighteenth-century standards of proportion and symmetry. Common to both for the past half-century has been the great movement toward simplicity, one that only recently has begun to give indications of a shift in direction.

This drive toward simplicity is itself a reaction to the excesses to which the Victorians carried the initial impetus of the eighteenth century.

It takes no expert to realize that the greatest godsend to the designers of home appliances in recent history was the discovery in aerodynamics of the value of the teardrop shape to the reduction of wind resistance. Streamlining was adopted with functional logic for vehicles in the various transportation fields first, and then was applied, without functional logic, to stationary household appliances ranging from the stove, refrigerator, and washing machine down

Best of all, streamlining suggested its own ethical justification. It was advertised as symbolizing the modern American's enlightened determination to cast off the encumbrances of convention in order to forge a new, vital, and dynamic civilization. Of course, once designers had sold business leaders on the importance of ethical justification to support styling appeal, it got to be a habit. A leading industrial designer told me recently that most of his clients were not satisfied when he merely presented a design for their product which they or surveyed consumers found attractive. They demanded an ethic for it. "So," he went on, "we give them an ethic. Ethic? That's a fashion, too."

As anyone who looks at the advertisements knows, however, the streamlining of many household appliances has abruptly ceased in the last few years. The new refrigerators are almost all rectilinear with severely sharp edges; the fully rounded sides have disappeared. Fashion, unable to exploit streamlining indefinitely, did not permit a gradual lessening of the curves and bulges but demanded a jump to the geometric block shape.

Other recent alterations following the same principles have been the desertion of pristine, sanitary white enameling in favor of an outburst of color, and also an abandonment of hard metallic or vitreous surfaces with a clinical look in favor of richer textures. Natural grained woods are being lavishly used for kitchen cabinets.

How does our theory of fashion leadership apply to automobile styling? The present turbulent state of affairs in the automobile market gives every indication that Poiret's nemesis of excess is once again in the process of making itself felt with decisive impact. This impact is portentous of great change for the shape and dimensions of the car body. This is evidenced not only by the current striking symptoms of shifts in the public's tastes but by what Detroit designers are saying and doing themselves.

Automotive stylists are thoroughly aware that the dynamics of styling in their industry correspond closely with the experience of other industries. A representative statement of their views can be found in a recent talk delivered by William M. Schmidt, executive stylist of the Chrysler Corporation:

The low silhouette is the most important and universal key to contemporary design. Low, ranch-type houses are in demand. Low, modern furniture is handsome, comfortable, and popular. More and more household appliances are being designed with the low look in mind. Modern office buildings, hotels, shopping centers, and civic and cultural centers are being designed for the eye appeal of low parallel lines, rather than the vertical lines of another styling era. To fit into its surroundings gracefully, the automobile also must have a contemporary appearance.

It is extremely interesting in this connection to note that of recent years the styling divisions of the automobile manufacturers have established regular channels of communication with key people in the women's fashion trades, although so far the guidance they have sought has largely been confined to interior styling and color and does not, as yet, appear to have been extended to the modeling of the body, the most important phase of exterior styling.

Detroit's decision to join the designers of household appliances in deserting streamlining for a relatively squared-off, boxy look—a decision that became apparent no later than 1954—is already past history and seems to have settled the question of contour for some time to come.

So there is no question about Detroit's awareness of general style trends. Yet, as Detroit looks ahead of its model-conversion and production lead times, it sees a major dilemma in styling policy:

¶ Stylists recognize that the extreme limits on lowness imposed by the human physique are only a few inches away (in the neighborhood of 45 inches) and will come close to realization in the 1960 models. These models are already predetermined beyond anything more than superficial changes.

¶ It also seems unquestionable that the long-established styling tendency toward longer overhang cannot practicably be carried much further. The analogy between this squashing effect and the tight lacing of the waist and the expansion of the skirt in the crinoline era is almost irresistible.

¶ In the same context, the tail fin—supposedly derived from the airplane tail—may be interpreted as a last resort of overextension, an outcropping that, quite seriously, serves much the same purpose as the bustle or the train. Although advertising claims have been made to the effect that fins serve the functional purpose of stabilizing a moving car in a cross wind, I found few designers in Detroit willing to say there is much scientific support for these claims.

What should Detroit do now? If it cannot go much further forward, should it gradually retrace its footsteps? I think not. Having utilized gradual compression and lengthwise expansion of the body as a means of differentiating new-model cars from old for so many years, it would

be entirely self-defeating for the industry to start building them a few inches shorter or higher, say, in 1961. The reason? This would be tantamount to repeating the dimensional style characteristics of 1957 or 1958. The new cars would then be duplicates of silhouettes already cluttering up the used-car lot, the last place Detroit wants to wind up.

As a matter of fact, the accuracy of this view has already been tested. In 1953 several models were introduced with bodies which were, in defiance of the main drift, *slightly* reduced in length. And the results, marketwise, were most unfortunate.

It is all too easy to misinterpret the significance that the soaring popularity of foreign cars holds as an index of shifts taking place in the tastes of the car-buying public. The unlikelihood that the representative American family will ever be satisfied with a really small car is not so much a question for the style analyst as a matter of cold reason.

In the first place, the size of the typical European car is, after all, an accident of the European economy and tax laws. In the United States smallness has undoubtedly been welcomed as a novelty, but like all novelties it will wear off in time. Secondly, while the future may well hold a comfortable niche for the pint-size model as a second car (free, incidentally, of the taint of the used-car lot) or as a special purpose vehicle, nevertheless only 12 per cent of American motorists own two automobiles. In addition, this is a big country, where more money is spent on touring than on any other form of recreation. Such factual considerations point to the conclusion that the standard model will have to remain sizable. (This does *not* mean, however, that it may not be made more compact.)

There are, then, many symptoms suggesting directions in which the taste of the automotive public is groping. Their very vitality attests to their significance. It was Poiret, too, who always insisted that in matters of fashion it is the consumer rather than the designer or producer who is the ultimate arbiter. To try to understand the complex problem of evolving automobile design without paying heed to what is happening in this world of car hobbyists would be a misguided effort.

The new interest in antique cars points toward a revival of forms comparable to those that have not been seen since the early days of motoring. Spurred on by, but also benefiting from, its foreign competition, Detroit will look back for inspiration to its own great heritage, not as a musty copybook of bygone designs to follow slavishly, but as a treasury of suggestions to be blended with modern concepts and technical innovations. And, considering the role the human memory plays in governing the timing of fashion swings, it probably would be wise for today's designers to re-examine the vintages of not merely one but two generations past.

Indeed, the theory of fashion leaves no choice but to conclude that, barring only the unlikely contingency that the automobile body is abandoned as a medium of fashion appeal, there must shortly ensue a striking reorientation of the shape and silhouette of American cars. In the decade ahead they should show a pronounced tendency to move away from their present attenuated appearance toward something less sleek but more commodious and comfortable.

Summing up, the force of fashion's fundamental reactions between the extremes of simplicity and elaboration or horizontality and verticality are suggestive of basic shifts in the design of the American car. The unsuitability of gradual reverses in fashion trends suggests that when these shifts set in, they are bound to be sharp and decisive. We are moving toward ornamentation and stateliness and probably veering toward the upright look once more. Finally, if the lessons of experience in the styling changes of other products are to be repeated, the transformation which lies ahead will be implemented both by a wave of functional innovation and by a revival movement.

Detroit stylists are already looking in this direction, despite the advertisements and public relations releases dedicated to help sell the current models. I was interested to discover during a recent Detroit visit that any number of the designers there are not only avidly interested in the early history of automobiling but are also well-versed authorities on models of the past. None of them, for example, expressed any astonishment when I raised the question of the likelihood of a revival movement. It would, of course, be misleading to create the impression that Detroit has been thinking explicitly along the lines outlined in this article. No outside observer can expect to be vouchsafed the innermost secrets of any company's styling policy.

Design is an artistic and therefore a largely intuitive process, and automobile design is no exception. It is by no means visionary to foresee the possibility that the art historian of an unborn generation may look back to our automobile bodies as the United States' most meaningful aesthetic achievement in plastic expression during the mid-twentieth century. The new cars are bound to be, insofar as the concept of newness can be meaningfully defined at all, new. It will doubtless take a practiced observer to detect in them the fusion of traditional images and functional advance that our interpretation anticipates.

My aim has been to provide a springboard to a better understanding of a fascinating but perplexing area of decision making. I have sought to point out that fashion—the impulse underlying the dynamics of style—is both a less mystifying and a more profound force in social behavior than is commonly supposed. Most authorities on fashion consider it an evolutionary process. In this I join them. Yet evolution relies on sudden mutations as much as, if not more than, small changes. For this reason, I have emphasized the sharply pronounced reactions which always seem to follow the extremes of styling.

Of course, I do not intend to put forward a formula or nostrum for the automatic prediction of style trends. History does not repeat itself any more neatly and prettily in styles than it does in any other sphere—business fluctuations, for example. My objective has been only to present a systematic exposition of a few of the insights that have long been the guideposts of fashion's most adept practitioners.

Nobody's crystal ball can show up the fashion future in complete detail. If it could, a lot of brain power would be unemployed; a lot of fun would go out of life. But this much is certain: the fact that an industry invests billions of dollars in equipment is no guarantee of a continued market for its products. Fashion is absolutely and callously indifferent to any monumental achievements in manufacturing proficiency. If anything, she takes capricious delight in nullifying man's industry, or pretenses to rationality. All of the fame and bulk of a leading textile, appliance, construction, or automobile company will not save it from fashion's dustbin if she so wills. She, and not the so-called fashion dictator—as Paul Poiret always professed—is the true autocrat; and only in a totalitarian state, where the consumer's taste is legislated by government edict, does she meet her match.

---

*The foregoing article appeared in the* Harvard Business Review *for November-December 1958, from which it is reprinted by permission. Its author, Dwight E. Robinson, teaches at the College of Business Administration, University of Washington.*

# Ten Authors in Pursuit of One Subject

CONTINUED FROM PAGE 17

other is a student nurse, a darling girl who is seduced—not by the doctor—in the back seat of an old convertible, parked in a drive-in theater. The chapter about the seduction is peculiarly effective because of the author's treatment: he describes the event in the same spirit and almost the same language he employs in describing the doctor's exploits with his Delahaye 235. Babs, the darling girl, is presented as a delicate racing machine, and her seducer as a sort of chauffeur-mechanic.

But isn't there at least a hint of the same attitude in all these novels? With two or three exceptions they are not about love as it used to be yearned for and celebrated. There is a pair of lovers in *Home from the Hill*; there is another in *Water Music* by Bianca VanOrden; in *The Fume of Poppies* there are Wendy Allen and her Lambie, who love each other long enough to make the book appealing in spite of its absurdities. In the other novels, however, there is almost nothing of love in the old sense of the word; there are no ideals, no self-sacrifices, no chivalry or even tenderness (but instead a sort of hearty, good-palsmanship), no social sanctions, no sense of guilt. There isn't even much passion (except Master Sergeant Callan's consuming passion for Private Tom Swanson, in Dennis Murphy's *The Sergeant*). Chiefly there is sex, and it is presented as an essentially mechanical process of action and reaction or stimulus and response.

All this creates a problem for the novelist. I am not thinking of the moral problem, but simply of the fiction writer's dilemma. If sex is regarded as a mechanical process, how can he write a new and deeply moving novel about it? How can he write at much greater length than the author, for example, of a mechanic's handbook for the latest Buick? He finds himself robbed of sentiments and words at every point in the story.

Take the essential seduction scene or sequence that goes back to the beginnings of fiction and far back into mythology. In the middle years of the eighteenth century Samuel Richardson devoutly believed that the seduction of a virtuous person was the blackest of sins. He wrote two novels about it, and one of them—*Clarissa Harlowe*—was in seven volumes. After the first four, the reader still didn't know whether Clarissa was going to keep her virtue. In the fifth volume she lost it; in the sixth and seventh she died of shame, and her penitent seductor was killed in a duel. The gradual weakening and shortening of the seduction sequence can be traced in the literature of the two centuries that followed. As late as 1948 Truman Capote was able to write a novel, *Other Voices, Other Rooms*, on that single theme, but it was a short novel, and in order to achieve an effect of tragic horror, he had to make the seduction homosexual.

I doubt whether any writer of the new generation could produce a seduction novel; the problem today is how to write a seduction scene of more than a few short paragraphs. Shirley Ann Grau manages to write thirteen pages in *The Hard Blue Sky* but only by introducing a flirtation with another woman and a narrowly averted homicide. Terry Southern writes ten effective pages by using his implied mechanical parallel. Bianca VanOrden has a three-and-a-half page seduction scene in the first chapter of *Water Music*, and it is notable because she transforms passion and wickedness into farce. The object of the attempt is Tosh Vorse, a talented young poet of indeterminate sex. The wicked seducer is a big-hearted, intense, and awkward young woman. Finding herself alone with Tosh for a moment, Cally flings herself at his head and topples him backward on a couch. Then as they wrestle, with Tosh weakened by laughter, she pants in his ear, "I desire you! I do! I do!"—because though Cally truly adores him, she is afraid to use the word *love*.

The characters in other novels are also afraid to use the word, and unlike poor Cally, they do not even think in terms of love. Most of them do not think at all; they merely have sensations. The result is that seduction scenes are usually confined to businesslike reports of sensations and behavior, written as if for an automotive handbook. Sometimes the whole process of enticement and surrender is dismissed in a page or less, and then the author is faced with the problem of what he is going to say in the rest of the chapter. The answer he finds may be numerical, with the first seduction followed by a second and even by a third. It is fair to say that many of these novelists have a weakness for purely numerical effects. Thus, in *The Fume of Poppies*, the author assumes that if it is shocking for Wendy to deceive her Lambie with one man, it is twice as shocking for her to deceive him with two men in one bed; perhaps he is right. In *Entry E* the drunken nymph becomes the half-willing prey of five students (one of the gang having incapacitated himself with whisky). But if five, why not ten or fifty, to multiply the effect?

"Why not?" a young writer named Ivan Gold must have asked himself while he was still a student at Columbia. In a story called "A Change of Air," published in the college literary magazine and reprinted in the fourth issue of *New World Writing*, he presented what may be the final metamorphosis of Clarissa Harlowe. His heroine is a factory girl who pays a visit to friends at the headquarters of an East Side gang, the Werewolves. During the next three days, the author says, "Bobbie Bedner (although expressing some desire to leave about four o'clock of the same afternoon when the situation seemed to be getting out of hand) nevertheless was taken, or rather had, one hundred and sixty times during seventy hours by a total of fifty-three persons." It was Bobbie herself who kept the tally. Although she slept only seven hours during the three days and nights and lost eleven pounds, she felt no resentment toward the Werewolves. She lived in a world where all emotions, including resentment, had given place to statistics. The story, published six years ago, still holds a sort of statistical championship, one that I hope is never challenged.

Sex in fiction has always been surrounded with social and moral values. Subtract those values from it and sex becomes a narrow subject, as easily exhausted as a single vein of ore. The author who deals with sex as a mechanical process is forced to depend on the one value of surprise: of going further than anyone has gone before; of using words that no one else has used in print (if any such remain); or of presenting situations that haven't been described except in textbooks of abnormal psychology. Even those extreme situations can usually be resolved into statistics— as in Bobbie Bedner's case—or else into plane geometry.

There is a triangle: two persons are competing with each other for sexual possession of a third. In the old American triangle, the Poor Boy and the Rich Boy, or Good Guy and Bad Guy—let us call them $M_1$ and $M_2$—form the base of the diagram, and they are competing for the love of $F_1$, the Boss's Daughter or the Bosomy Doll. In another American triangle, revealing the new sexual aggressiveness of women, F1 and F2, the Secretary and the Heiress, are competing for the love of M1, the Boss.

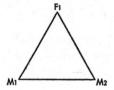 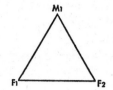

By now these familiar situations offer only a limited opportunity for surprise or shock. But the triangle can always be inverted by a process known as the sexual switcheroo. New relationships, usually incestuous, can be introduced among the characters, and then we have the sexual snapper. Here are a few examples of the switcheroo and the snapper among recent books by the younger novelists:

*The Sergeant*, by Dennis Murphy. We are offered a simple inversion of the triangle: M1 and F1 are struggling for total possession of M2. In this case M1 is Master Sergeant Callan, a tyrant in his little kingdom; F1 is a wisely understanding French girl; and M2, the apex of the triangle, is a handsome private. The book has authority in spite of its dealing with a familiar situation; Murphy can write. The master sergeant, struggling against his passion and devouring himself like a wounded hyena, becomes a tragic rather than a merely pathetic figure.

*Parktilden Village*, by George P. Elliott. There is a handsome sociologist at the apex of the triangle, and there are two women, both his mistresses, at the base. The snapper is that F1 is the mother of F2. But *Parktilden Village* has other distinctions besides an entertaining style: it is the only one of the ten novels that has a villain (the sociologist) and the only one that leads to a religious conclusion, after the daughter's life has been ruined. The trouble is that Elliott describes juvenile delinquency and the scabrous behavior of the sociologist with more gusto than he shows in reporting the religious conversion of the girl's parents. In the end he seems to be pulling God out of a hat.

*Water Music*, by Bianca VanOrden. The story begins with the same inverted triangle that appears in *The Sergeant*, but the author has a snapper to add. At the apex of the triangle is Tosh Vorse, a young poet of immense promise; at the base are Bayard, a homosexual composer, and Cally, who teaches art in a girls' school. Bayard has seduced Tosh three years before the book opens, and Cally seduces him in the first chapter. The snapper is that Bayard and Cally are brother and sister. Tosh loves neither of them; what he truly loves is writing poetry. He becomes entranced, however, with one of Cally's pupils, Laura Beasley, whose ambition to do something great is equal to his own. Cally

finds a second-best suitor, and Bayard will disappear with others of his kind, so that the triangle becomes a solid rectangle. Besides her sense of form and her gift for comedy, Miss VanOrden has an almost unique ability to present a poet whose talent is documented and believable.

*Heroes and Orators*, by Robert Phelps. Here the apex of the triangle is Elizabeth, an intensely and distributively heterosexual young woman—a "fish," as the author tells us her type is called in Lesbian circles. The figures at the base are Margot, a protective older woman, and Roger, the narrator, who wants to join the happy throng of Elizabeth's lovers. But Roger has a pregnant wife and also a tough male cousin whom Elizabeth prefers as a bedmate, so that the triangle becomes a pentagon before dissolving into shapeless confusion.

Once the process of inverting the triangle and changing the figures at its base and apex has been reduced to a diagram, it becomes simple to introduce new variations. Instead of mother and daughter fighting over a common lover, as in *Parktilden Village* (and some other recent novels), why not father and daughter? Perhaps that has been done already—but why not a triangle with grandmother and granddaughter at the base of it? Grandmothers have been neglected in sexual fiction. Or why not use a suggestion from Apuleius and have a triangle composed of husband, wife, and donkey—perhaps transformed into a rectangle when the donkey falls in love with an adulterous she-mule? If you can't play it for shocks, then play it for laughs. Very soon *Lolita* will be inverted in a novel about a middle-aged woman with a passion for vicious little boys: faunets.

Did I make the mistake of saying "very soon?" I forgot that a novel with the inverted plot was published in 1950: *The Roman Spring of Mrs. Stone*, by Tennessee Williams. The sexual potentialities of the human being are so rigidly limited that every situation and combination has already been described in some form of literature. The younger novelists were deluding themselves when they imagined that sex was a new territory in fiction, where homesteads could be staked out as in the Cherokee Strip. On a given day they gathered at the border, waiting for a signal gun and meanwhile cursing the Sooners who had stolen into the territory before the legal moment—damn that Henry Miller for printing his books in Paris!—then the gun was fired at noon, and the dusty mob streamed forward, looking for land. What they found in this case was chiefly abandoned farm lands with most of the topsoil gone. I imagine that the best of the younger novelists—and they are talented—will soon be moving on to richer fields.

*A member of America's youngest literary generation in the Paris of the 1920's, Mr. Cowley has been ever since the publication in 1934 of his* Exile's Return *a leading critic, editor, and historian of letters at home. His writings include the survey* The Literary Situation. *Last year he edited the anthology* Writers at Work.

# What Not to See in Europe

CONTINUED FROM PAGE 85

done in front of the customer in the dining room, instead of where it should be—in the kitchen.

Almost every country has its culinary foolishness. The *Grand Prix* of silly specialties goes to *crêpes Suzette*, which has made millionaires out of pretentious captains. The customers tip him royally for his impressive juggling of liqueur bottles but they forget that the *crêpes*, the basic element, were made outside in the kitchen by an anonymous man who gets no tip. Austria's cooks have contributed *Salzburger Nockerln*, a *soufflé* in the form of a small mountain. And the English, renowned for their ability to ruin fine foodstuffs, have taken credit for inventing the trifle, an unfathomable sweet nonsense.

Certain dishes, like certain wines, don't travel well. I cannot explain why spaghetti tastes so well in Italy but never outside the country; it must be the sun, or the air, or the preparation. (French bread is never French and crusty in the French restaurants of New York.) A simple *omelette aux fines herbes*, that masterpiece of French cooking, has never been reproduced perfectly outside of France. *Smörgåsbord* is an exciting adventure in a good restaurant in Sweden but often a dreadful affair elsewhere when it becomes merely a convenient excuse to serve leftovers. Brook trout *au bleu* should never be ordered

more than ten miles away from the brook where it was caught. And there ought to be a law that *bouillabaisse* may be served only in restaurants from whose front door you can see the sea and smell the scent of the incoming tide.

Instead of an epilogue, here are a few random discommendations for this year's traveler:

Dilapidated castles, particularly in Austria, Germany, and France, run as hostelries by dilapidated members of the local aristocracy. Some modern plumbing, many old walls, and high-class snobbism at scandalous prices.

Tourist attractions that thrive on the macabre: Madame Tussaud's gruesome waxworks in London; Hitler's former residence near Berchtesgaden; the battlefield of Waterloo in Belgium; the Tower of London.

The highways of northern Italy during the last two weeks in August, the traditional *fer' agosto*, when almost all Italians seem to be driving on the road, at high speed.

Rural buses in Ireland. They have to be seen to be believed. It is not true that the passengers are a happy, carefree lot, as you might have expected after reading Irish short stories.

Sights that violate the standards of good taste: Rome's Palazzo Venezia (when something goes wrong in Italy, it's a beaut); the horrible Stalin monument overlooking Prague; the Palace of Culture in Warsaw; Positano (the Capri of the 1950's).

Garmisch-Partenkirchen, a motorized American Army winter resort, extremely *ungemütlich*.

Railway station restaurants in England.

Naples—even Caruso's songs can't conceal the poverty and unhappiness of its inhabitants.

Harry's Bar in Venice, except when homesick for 52nd Street. (You will not find Hemingway there.)

Third-class tourist hotels in Spain.

Many second-class hotels in Spain.

Some supposedly first-class hotels in Spain.

You take it up from there. I could go on and on. But I admit that all these places and things have to be seen in order to be appreciated—which means that you must make your own Grand Tour in any case. The fatherly guides who wrote the old, red-backed Baedekers often used to set down beside the name of some city or site that they found not particularly worthwhile the forbidding phrase, "Nothing need detain the tourist here." Yet they never intended thereby to discourage tourists, and neither do I. They assumed the irresistible presence of tourists, even as one assumes the flood tides of spring. Suppose the flood dried up—a reversal that might affect the wellsprings of the world as well as our own knowledge of it—what then? Perish the thought. I only hope that a few molecules of the annual tourist surge may become pleasantly detained in less known eddies, rather than just float down the 3-O or 3-D main channels.

---

*Joseph Wechsberg has been for many years an intrepid traveler of Europe's highways and byways while writing on Continental subjects for American magazines. To the November, 1958, issue of* HORIZON *he contributed "Behind the Golden Curtain."*

# The World's Most Daring Builder

CONTINUED FROM PAGE 24

end, twenty-one buttresses along the enclosed rear of the building, and three great supports on the open front.

In the second series of hangars, begun at the start of World War II, Nervi profited from experience. Since he knew that he could make reinforced concrete act as powerfully as steel, he reasoned that he could also employ a standard technique of steel construction: prefabrication. He decided to precast the reinforced concrete members, and then to use them as if they were steel girders which had been made in a mill. This was a major breakthrough in the art of concrete construction. Nervi did not invent precasting, but he was the first to employ precast elements on this scale. In economic terms alone, compared with the earlier group of hangars, the rewards of his achievement were striking. The second scheme provided savings of 30 per cent in steel reinforcement, 35 per cent in concrete, and 60 per cent in form lumber. The dividend in beauty was even greater. These were perhaps the most dramatic structures of the first half of the twentieth century.

Their very erection was a performance of great brilliance. The ribs of reinforced concrete were hoisted in place by cranes. Their protruding metal rods were welded together, and grouted—that is, filled with cement mortar. In theory the entire structure thus became homogeneous. But Nervi worried about the joints. The tremendous structures were particularly sensitive to changes in temperature. Deformations occurred, which might have sent them crashing to the ground, had the design not provided for such contingencies. The hangars held, responding to sun and snow, and to wind, and correcting themselves as Nervi had hoped they would. The tremendous roofs were alive, and as an Italian critic has remarked, seemed merely attached to the earth by their supports, rather than held up by them. For, instead of the numerous buttresses which he used in the first group of hangars, Nervi here employed only six monumental supports, one at each corner, and one in the center of each long side.

But now Italy plunged into war. Nervi constructed underground storage tanks for crude oil, and concrete ships which remained unfinished as the tide turned in favor of the Allies. When the Italian effort collapsed, the Germans occupied the country as if it were a conquered nation. As they retreated, they dynamited every one of Nervi's hangars. The structures did not disintegrate but settled slowly to the ground like enormous wire cages. Nervi was heartbroken. Nevertheless, he inspected the ruins. The joints, for which he felt such concern, were still joined solidly in the rubble.

Nervi went into semiretirement during the German occupation, spending his time in artistic reflection and research. He perfected a new material which he named "ferro-cemento"—a quick-hardening and exceptionally durable concrete reinforced with fine steel mesh, rather than with rods, and capable of being cast in sheets less than an inch thick.

Ferro-cemento may prove to be Nervi's most profound contribution to the art of construction. Certainly it is one of the most versatile building materials yet devised by man. Here, too, early pioneers had prepared the way for Nervi. In the last century Cottancin was aware of the advantage of mesh reinforcement. The German architect Dominikus Böhm in 1926 vaulted his remarkable church at Neu-Ulm with precast mesh elements. But Böhm's material did not approach the quality of Nervi's, and his system of prefabrication did not open the stirring prospect, as Nervi's does, of the manufacture of concrete buildings by assembly-line methods. Eventually ferro-cemento may enable Nervi to construct the visionary edifice he sketched in 1943, a hall spanning almost 1,000 feet, which could easily cover the plaza of Saint Peter's of Rome. Already ferro-cemento has commenced to change the face of the world.

In 1947 Nervi built a small storehouse of ferro-cemento in his own construction yard so that he could examine its properties. He found that the walls, corrugated for the sake of stiffness, but only an inch and one-tenth thick, were perfectly stable. His first chance to use the material in a fairly sizable building came that year when he covered the swimming pool of the Naval Academy at Leghorn with a fifty-foot vault made up of hollow ferro-cemento elements through which warm air circulated. Later that year came the larger opportunity for which he had long been waiting.

Turin, the Detroit of Italy, urgently wished to rebuild its bomb-damaged exhibition hall. Once famous for its annual international automobile salon, the city was striving to regain its prominence in the European market. A new hall, in which cars and other industrial products could be displayed, was needed with all possible speed. But as usual, little money was available. When the Turin Exhibition Board held a competition, therefore, it came as no surprise that Nervi won. His bid was for the equivalent of $500,000, which even under Italian conditions was so low as to cause suspicion. Moreover, Nervi proposed to erect the great structure in a matter of months. He would use light, traveling formwork on which the precast elements of the roof would be placed by derricks. When a section of the roof had been completed, the forms, which were really a scaffolding rather than traditional formwork, would be lowered and moved on rails to the next section.

The members of the exhibition board, as they consulted with Nervi, could not help but wonder whether Nervi's plans were structurally sound. Could he refer them, they asked, to a completed building of a similar nature? Nervi of course could not; and it is characteristic of him that he

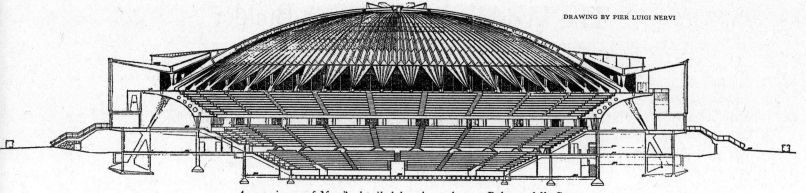

*As seen in one of Nervi's detailed drawings, the new Palazzo dello Sport
in Rome suggests the supple strength and ribbed delicacy of an umbrella.*

relates the episode as a tribute to the courage of his client. Of his own genius he says nothing, but it provided Turin with one of the most magnificent rooms in the history of architecture.

From either side of a nave 300 feet across, flight after flight of buttresses, their lean strength suggesting the flying arches of Gothic cathedrals, soar upward to receive the thrust of the great corrugated vault that spans the full width of the hall. The vault, serving as ceiling and roof, is one inch and a half thick. Through its hundreds of skylights, the sun enters the vast interior.

All is space and light, as it must be in great architecture. At the end overlooking the Po, the wall opens on the half-dome of a rotunda whose diameter of 132 feet is almost as great as that of the dome of the Florence cathedral or the Pantheon. Because the problems of vaulting the dome were different from those of the main room, Nervi naturally attacked them in a different manner. He created a fabric of nervations that have been compared with those of the *Victoria regia* water lily. The structure possesses a virtually biological form that is the true expression of the forces working within it, and which has the light complex grace of a flower.

Nervi now could accomplish whatever he wished in ferro-cemento. A series of extraordinary structures followed: a smaller exhibition hall at Turin, vaulted in the manner of the rotunda of the main hall, but oblong in form, and mounted on four splendid flattened arches that made leaps of more than 100 feet from corner to corner of the room; then a gay parasol of a beach pavilion at Ostia, spreading outward like a delicate plant from a central stem; two parabolic salt warehouses at Tortona, works of particular dignity and eloquence. At the spa of Chianciano he built a sober, quiet hall in which the mineral waters were to be taken, but the ceiling of the nearby ballroom was a brilliant sunflower bursting open with light.

This was an utterly human architecture, based as always on precise technical considerations, but also deeply considerate of man's functional needs and his civilized aspirations. Each building had its own logic and scale, its own exuber-

ance or tact. Nervi's quiet charm, his personal modesty, his humor, are all present in his work. Playfully he constructed the thirty-eight-foot ketch *Nennele* in 1948. Its hull is a "skin" structure, half an inch thick, made entirely of ferro-cemento. After a decade of cruising, it remains perfectly watertight, impervious to shocks and minor collisions, and very fast under sail.

Under his touch the new material opened countless structural possibilities. Nervi used it instead of wooden formwork, and proceeded to erect a group of remarkable factories with dazzling speed. In one hundred days he finished a Fiat plant nearly half a mile long by employing mobile ferro-cemento formwork at several levels simultaneously, the third floor advancing slightly behind the second, and the second slightly behind the first. Abstract compositions appeared on the ceilings of these plants, especially one suggested to Nervi by Aldo Arcangeli, at the Gatti wool factory in Rome, where the stresses moving through the floor slab are clearly revealed in the projecting ribs of ferro-cemento.

Without losing vigor, Nervi's designs acquired additional richness. The quality of nonstructural detail, too, became more distinguished in every way. The main reason for the improvement was that he was now collaborating with architects of the first rank. Previously Nervi had been content to work with mediocre architects, even in major commissions (as the nondescript exteriors of the Turin exposition halls reveal painfully). In the fifties, however, his collaborators often have been men of international stature, such as the American Marcel Breuer and Bernard Zehrfuss of France, with whom he executed one of the exciting commissions of the century: the UNESCO headquarters in Paris.

Yet the profound differences which separate Nervi from more formal architects are strikingly apparent in the group of UNESCO buildings. Breuer and Zehrfuss were dominant in designing the Secretariat building—an interesting piece of architecture, if only because of the unusual Y-plan which provides ever-changing vistas of the façades. Nevertheless a number of other architects—Le Corbusier, for example—might have designed an essentially similar structure.

The adjacent Conference Hall, on the other hand, is pure Nervi. The solid forward wall, pleated in monumental forms, was folded backward and downward at its summit to form an inclined corrugated roof. The roof slants down past the center of the building, and then rises again in asymmetrical balance, as it approaches the rear of the building, where it folds downward to form the rear wall. At its lowest point the roof is supported by a row of columns which are shaped like shards of crystal, rectangular at the top, elliptical at the bottom. Although they may appear to be sculpture, the columns are a pure structural expression of the forces flowing downward through them from the great roof. The sides of the building, which have no structural supporting task, have been treated as abstractions in glass and concrete.

Somehow it is fitting that this monument should belong to UNESCO and thus to the world. Nervi's work generally now belongs to mankind. His influence, direct or indirect, is taking effect in countries as widely separated as Argentina and Japan. In the United States he has acted as consultant on two noteworthy projects: a church by Breuer now being erected at St. John's University Abbey in Collegeville, Minnesota, whose folded structure suggests that of the UNESCO hall; and another monastic church at the Priory of St. Mary and St. Louis at Creve Coeur, Missouri—a triple-tiered circular structure of free-flowing thin shells by Hellmuth, Obata, & Kassabaum. Neither of these projects, in which Nervi's role has been very minor, possesses the distinction and strength of his own work in Europe. The churches are important chiefly because they reflect the awakening interest of American architects in revolutionary structural forms which, until the last decade, were almost completely ignored in this country.

Nervi, of course, has by no means been alone in developing the new structural idiom. Other designers are receiving long deserved world-wide recognition, too. The Spaniard Eduardo Torroja, author of the great Madrid hippodrome and the market at Algeciras, has made contributions to the science of reinforced concrete construction that in some ways are theoretically more significant than Nervi's, but he has never exploited the possibilities of precasting with the audacity of the Italian. Mexico's Félix Candela, who was born in Spain and studied under Torroja, has created shells of superlative grace; and in company with O'Neil Ford and several other American architects he has designed the thin-shell roofs and space-frame structure of the recently completed Texas Instruments plant at Dallas.

It is worth noting, however, that for so ambitious a project, a foreign structural designer was called to this country. For although men such as Candela and Nervi have shown that the no man's land between architecture and engineering is in reality the promised land of the art of building, the United States remains largely a desert so far as structural innovation is concerned. Only a handful of

designers are striving to abandon what Nervi scornfully calls "imitations of the solutions of the past." But sometimes the efforts of these Americans are impressive, as in the case of the projected assembly hall for the University of Illinois by Harrison & Abramovitz—a ribbed concrete saucer 400 feet in diameter which will be covered by a folded thin-shell dome. Engineers for this vast unobstructed arena are Amman and Whitney, one of the largest engineering firms in the country, whose leading designer, Boyd Anderson, is an adventurous figure in contemporary architecture. Truly outstanding work is being done by perhaps a dozen other architects and engineers, including Minoru Yamasaki, Fred Severud, Paul Wiedlinger, Milo Ketchum, and Nervi's former students Myron Goldsmith and James Ferris. Yet none has come close to equaling the accomplishments of the Italian master.

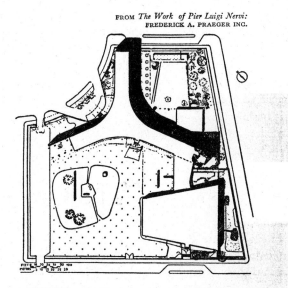

*At UNESCO's new Paris headquarters, jointly designed by Zehrfuss, Breuer, and Nervi, the latter worked primarily on the conference rooms at lower right.*

As he approaches seventy, Nervi continues steadfastly on his revolutionary path. Four new structures in Italy show him to be as bold, as eager to embrace untried ideas as ever before in his long career. With his distinguished countryman Gio Ponti he has constructed the thirty-story Pirelli skyscraper in Milan, one of the most powerfully conceived tall buildings in the world. Since structural steel, as can be expected in Italy, would have been prohibitively expensive in so large an undertaking, Nervi and Ponti relied exclusively on reinforced concrete. They devised a unique structure, wedge-shaped at either end, which is stabilized by four tapering cores of concrete that rise the full height of the building. The exterior façades are immense curtain walls of glass, which reveal the building's full structural brilliance when it is illuminated at night.

Simultaneously, in Rome, Nervi has executed his first great commissions in the city where he has practiced for nearly four decades. For the 1960 Olympic Games he has created three stadiums which are probably the most splendid ensemble of structures ever built for sporting events. The largest, designed in company with his architect-son Antonio, is an arena for field events that holds 50,000 spectators, 8,000 of them beneath a shell roof of prestressed concrete cantilevered outward above the central stand. The other two stadiums, intended for indoor sports, are entirely covered. They have given Nervi the opportunity to show the Eternal City, celebrated for its domes, how domes should be constructed in the middle of the twentieth century.

The smaller hall, or Palazzetto, which seats 5,000 for wrestling or boxing matches and 4,000 for tennis and basketball, was erected in forty days. Its circular vault, composed of precast elements of ferro-cemento, is the most beautiful of Nervi's sunflowers. Soaring upward on great Y-shaped buttresses, flying free of the earth in a single spontaneous gesture of confidence and ease, it spans a diameter of 194 feet. Michelangelo's dome of Saint Peter's spans fifty-seven feet less, and it would fall down if it were not held erect by chains, concealed within the construction, which have always been necessary to correct its instability. Michelangelo conceived architecture as sculpture. Nervi has never made that basic error. To its last detail his dome is a masterpiece of structural logic: *Non murato*, as Vasari wrote long ago,

*ma veramente nato*—"not merely built, but truly born."

Although the Palazzetto is one of Nervi's most brilliant creations, it is overshadowed by the nearly completed Palazzo—a great hall seating 15,000—which is the culminating triumph of the Olympic group. This tremendous amphitheater, walled by curving expanses of glass, is covered by a dome more than 300 feet in diameter: about three times the span of the dome of Hagia Sophia, more than twice that of the Pantheon and Saint Peter's. The apex of the dome—110 feet above the playing surface—is about the same height as the vault of Notre Dame of Paris. From the center the ribs of the undulating ceiling descend like radii, alive with light from lamps concealed within its corrugated, windowed elements. At the perimeter, in groups of three, the ribs meet fan-shaped buttresses which transmit the thrust of the dome through the stands below in long inclined piers. These supports, shaped like long twisting spindles, shoot downward through the spacious concourses, which next summer will be thronged by visitors from all nations, for whom the vast and honest structure was meant by its designer.

---

*Allan Temko, a student of architecture and history now teaching at the University of California at Berkeley, contributed the article "The Flowering of San Francisco" to the January, 1959, HORIZON.*

# "The Greatest Wit in England"

CONTINUED FROM PAGE 95

was roused. Mrs Partington's spirit was up. But I need not tell you that the contest was unequal. The Atlantic Ocean beat Mrs Partington.

He now had to reside for part of every year in London, which of course delighted him, and take the services at St. Paul's. His friends wished to hear him preach, but he did his best to dissuade them, warning one of them: "Do not flatter yourself with the delusive hope of a slumber. I preach violently, and there is a strong smell of sulphur in my sermons." His fellow clergy might have preferred sulphur to satire, for when it was proposed that St. Paul's should be surrounded by a wooden pavement they failed to laugh heartily at his suggestion: "Let the Dean and Canons lay their heads together, and the thing will be done."

He was beginning to suffer from gout, which he described as "the only enemy that I do not wish to have at my feet," and from the effects of living too well. To his old friend Murray he wrote: "Having ascertained the weight of what I could live upon, so as to preserve health and strength, and what I did live upon, I found that, between ten and seventy years of age, I had eaten and drunk forty four-horse wagon-loads of meat and drink more than would have preserved me in life and health. The value of this mass of nourishment I considered to be worth seven thousand pounds sterling. It occurred to me that I must, by my voracity, have starved to death fully a hundred persons. This is a frightful calculation, but irresistibly true; and I think, dear Murray, your wagons would require an additional horse each!"

The hay fever still troubled him in the summer months: "My fear is of perishing by deliquescence—I melt away in nasal and lachrymal profluvia. . . . The membrane is so irritable that light, dust, contradiction, an absurd remark, the sight of a Dissenter—anything, sets me sneezing; and if I begin sneezing at twelve, I don't leave off till two o'clock, and am heard distinctly at Taunton when the wind sets that way, at a distance of six miles."

He hailed the coming of the railway to Bristol with rapture; he could now reach London without having to spend two nights on the road, and without being shaken until his bones ached. Yet such was the natural inefficiency of men that no improvements were made in the safety of travel unless accidents forced them upon the railway company. "Every fresh accident on the railroads is an advantage, and leads to an improvement," he told Murray. "What we want is an overturn which would kill a bishop, or at least a dean. This mode of conveyance would then become perfect."

The great days of Holland House were almost over. Sheridan and his set had given place to Macaulay and Dickens. Sydney was still the chief wit, with Macaulay as long-distance talker. At last, in 1840, the famous reign of epigrams and hospitality passed away with the death of Lord Holland, and Sydney wrote dolefully: "It is indeed a great loss to me; but I have learned to live as a soldier does in war, expecting that on any one moment the best and the dearest may be killed before his eyes. . . . I have gout, asthma, and seven other maladies, but am otherwise very well." His ailments did not prevent him from dining out. Preferring dull society to no society at all, he remained calm when his fun missed fire: "I must do her the justice to say that when my jokes are explained to her, and she has leisure to reflect upon them, she laughs very heartily." A Frenchman, who wished to write about his work, applied to him for biographical material. He gave it: "I am much given to talking, laughing, and noise. I dine with the rich in London, and physic the poor in the country; passing from the sauces of Dives to the sores of Lazarus."

He wrote and published a series of letters on ecclesiastical matters, which infuriated the bishops, and the projected disestablishment of the Scotch Church drew this from him: "Before I form any opinion on Establishments, I should like to know the effects they produce on vegetables. Many of our clergy suppose that if there was no Church of England, cucumbers and celery would not grow; that mustard and cress could not be raised. If Establishments are connected so much with the great laws of nature, this makes all the difference; but I cannot believe it." From such weighty themes, he would turn to give advice to a friend, such as this to Lady Holland: "I think you mistake Bond's character in supposing he could be influenced by partridges. He is a man of very independent mind, with whom pheasants at least, or perhaps turkeys, are necessary."

Many people, including Macaulay, testified that Sydney did not reserve his good sayings for the tables of the rich, but that his chief pleasure was to keep his wife and family in fits of laughter for hours on end. He never expressed his true nature more completely than in a letter he wrote to Jeffrey: "The haunts of Happiness are varied, and rather unaccountable; but I have more often seen her among little children, and home firesides, and in country houses, than anywhere else—at least I think so."

In 1844 it seemed to him that he had not long to live; his heart was beginning to trouble him, he had fits of giddiness, and he experienced difficulty in breathing and moving. "I saw the other day," he wrote to his doctor, "a ball of fire, with a tail as long as the garden, rush across the heavens and descend towards the earth. That it had some allusion to me and my affairs I did not doubt, but could not tell what, till I found the cow had slipped her calf: this made all clear." He suffered much from languor and sadly confessed: "I feel so weak both in body and mind that

I verily believe, if the knife were put into my hand, I should not have strength or energy enough to slide it into a Dissenter."

Illness gained upon him and he traveled to London. Here he was sternly dieted, and from his bed he wrote: "If you hear of sixteen or eighteen pounds of human flesh, they belong to me. I look as if a curate had been taken out of me." He informed Lady Grey that he was comfortably installed in a suite of rooms "perfectly fitted up for illness and death." One of his last acts was to bestow a living on a poor clergyman who was "an out-and-out Tory." There was a flash of the old humor at the very end. Searching for his medicine, the nurse found half a bottle of ink in the

THE BRITISH MUSEUM

*This sketch of Smith was made by the Irish painter Daniel Maclise.*

place where it ought to have been, and said jokingly that he had probably taken a dose of ink the previous time by mistake. "Then bring me all the blotting paper there is in the house," said Sydney. He died on the twenty-second of February, 1845.

Few people search for truth among lapidary inscriptions; yet Sydney's epitaph at Kensal Green does him no more than justice. He was "One of the Best of Men."

*Well known over the past quarter century as a biographer of vigorous creative spirits, Hesketh Pearson numbers among his portrait gallery Dickens and Oscar Wilde, Whistler and Conan Doyle, Erasmus Darwin and Bernard Shaw—about whom he wrote in the November, 1958, HORIZON.*

# Miró <small>CONTINUED FROM PAGE 78</small>

native qualities constantly run the risk of entering into conflict with the foreign styles taken over as a result of Catalonia's no less native internationalism and curiosity. For Catalan art to flourish, foreign style and hereditary traits must coincide. This had happened in the case of the Romanesque, but Catalonia's vigorous extravagance had not found another real outlet until the birth of a style at the turn of the last century variously known as *art nouveau* or *Jugendstil*. When this did occur, it resulted at once in the emergence of a creator greatly admired by Miró: the architect Gaudí.

Salvador Dali, another Catalonian, has said of his countrymen: "All Catalonians are paranoiacs." Gaudí, in the course of his fairly long life, completed only a dozen major projects, but they amply testify to the violence and inventiveness of his eccentricity. The columns of his houses erupt like eucalyptus trees; their façades are corroded by a rash of bright ceramic splinters assembled into mosaics; their balconies are overgrown with iron vines; and the chimneys on their roofs are like monstrous bubbles that never manage to burst. In the Park Güell in Barcelona, Gaudí gives free rein to his imagination. Irregularity is the law. Pillars and walls bulge, sway, sprout huge chancres and stalactites, assume delirious anthropomorphic shapes. Pyramids are poised on their tips, colonnades lean enough to make the Tower of Pisa seem straight in comparison. Everywhere, profusion and planned anarchy prevail.

To materialize his fancies, Gaudí resorted to bold, often prophetic means. When the local ceramic workers went on strike, Gaudí bought quantities of old ceramics, smashed them into bits, and reassembled the pieces in what are probably the first collages in the history of art. As Miró and the surrealists were to do a generation or two later, Gaudí used odds and ends in his creations: shells from the nearby beach, scraps from the textile mill for which he was building a church. Miró himself recently confided to Camilo José

Cela: "Everything that comes out of the earth is good." Gaudí, who shared this faith, affirmed that the source of his aberrant inventions was not gratuitous fantasy but nature. His claim is justified, for the landscape of Catalonia can vie in extravagance with the richest imagination. The bizarre shapes of the rocks of Montserrat, the boil-like cacti and bulging calabashes of Montroig would seem to indicate that the divinity that presided over the formation of this land belonged to the same eccentric lineage as Gaudí and Miró.

These are the real roots that fed Miró's magic flowers. But roots are invisible; from 1923 onward, Miró appeared to be a true member and product of the School of Paris. There he lived and worked unobtrusively, with the exception of frequent, indispensable trips to his native Catalonia. From one of these, in 1929, he came back married. Underneath, his work as well as his life unfolded in a simple line. It was sometimes deflected but never broken by external influences. Miró was like a Captain Nemo who had dived deep into his own element; the disturbances on the surface affected him only distantly. One can discern phases in his mature career, but they are so fluid and pliant that dating and classifying them is as hopeless as trying to capture water in a sieve. His art, like a plant at the bottom of the ocean, sways in the currents but remains fundamentally unaltered. For a while Miró practiced pure automatism as advocated by the surrealists. Soon, however, a horde of neatly described if unidentifiable monsters invaded his stage. In the early thirties, geometrical abstraction reached its high water mark, and Miró was influenced by the painters Mondrian, Léger, and Arp; his forms became less anecdotal, his compositions more severe. Even so, he remained himself. You sense that under his brush Euclid's triangles are always dying to play hooky.

In 1936 the specter of civil war rose over Spain. Again Miró was affected: his fantastic scenes became anguished, oppressive; the dreams turned into nightmare. When the

Second World War broke out, Miró left Paris for Varengeville, a little fishing harbor on the Channel. A year later France collapsed; all life, private and public, was precipitated into chaos. Taking along his fragile crew of sprites, Miró sought shelter amidst the stars—or rather behind them. In the cacophony of a demented world, his *Constellations* captured an echo of the music of the spheres.

In 1940 Miró moved back to Spain, where he has lived ever since, dividing his time between Montroig, Barcelona, and Palma, with an occasional visit to Paris. When the war ended and Miró's art reappeared on the international scene, it was evident that something in it had changed again. The elements that peopled Miró's painting had turned from things into signs. They no longer composed a world, but a language. It is as when we teach a child to count by lining up objects before him. At first, he is aware only of the pipe, the pencil, the apple. Then, gradually, the notion of one, two, three becomes clear to him; and as it does, the actual presence of the objects gives way to the abstract idea which they convey.

Progress, for signs, lies in clarity and elegance of formulation. At first sharp and minute, Miró's writing became looser, more dashing; it now had the sovereign nonchalance, the decorative appeal of Oriental calligraphy. Still, the substance *of* which the signs are made cannot change greatly; but the substance *on* which they are written can. The backgrounds of Miró's pictures have become richer and more varied, sometimes hard as ice, sometimes soft and porous as blotting paper. His harmonies are more extreme and acid than ever. In his search for new supports for his tested signs, Miró has turned to lithography, to sculpture, and most of all to ceramics—his culminating effort in this technique being the two walls completed this winter for the new UNESCO building in Paris. Miró had redeemed the material world as he saw it by giving it his imagination; it has now paid him back by lending him its density.

Ten years ago, in one of his few written statements, Miró declared: "I dream that, when I shall be able to settle down somewhere, I shall have a very large studio, not for reasons of lighting, to which I am indifferent, but in order to have a great deal of room, many canvases, for the more I work the more I feel like working." Miró's dream has come true. Two years ago he moved into a vast, radiantly immaculate studio built for him, on the terrace beneath his villa near Palma de Majorca, by the Catalan architect José Luis Sert. Below there is an almond grove, which in January explodes into white blossoms; there is the warm, rocky earth of Majorca; there is the sea. Streaming in through doors and windows comes the light of Majorca —that light which, as Miró says, "is saturated with purest poesy; it reminds me of the light of those oriental things which appear as if seen through a veil, the light of those meticulous things which are drawn. . . . " The landscape, the light—"these things," Miró told me, "keep my soul in shape, as calisthenics do my body."

Here Miró has set himself to work, surrounded by a thousand and one objects that help him to project himself into his thousand and one nights: butterflies, starfish, a bull's head and a sun's head made of straw, the skeleton of a bat, a contraption called "The Eighth Marvel of the World" which turns out to contain a jack-in-the-box, insects ("they are signs made by earth"), a miniature farmyard, a pitchfork, African *tapas* and aboriginal bark paintings, a "moon fish" (perhaps Nature's most Miróesque creation), zoomorphic jars from the nearby island of Ibiza, a gracefully jagged piece of rubber tire, gourds, broken pots and pans—an abundant harvest of flotsam and jetsam gathered on walks through field, street, and beach. Adjusted by the artist's hand or simply dropped in a corner, these odds and ends wake up, as if touched by a fairy's wand, to become citizens of Miróland. Here he has begun to work—on many projects at once, as is his custom. "I shall mix large and small formats. It will be a real *salade*. I am going to make immense things. Two years from now, one won't be able to move any more." And he adds: "I feel that I am on the brink of a very brutal evolution. I feel that I shall now be able to paint things that I could not have painted three years ago." Another new leaf? It would not be in the least astonishing, coming from one who is the master of perpetual metamorphosis and rejuvenation.

ILLUSTRATIONS FROM *Joan Miró: His Graphic Work* BY SAM HUNTER, RECENTLY PUBLISHED BY HARRY N. ABRAMS, INC., NEW YORK

*Pierre Schneider, an American free-lance writer living in Paris, is a correspondent for* Art News. *He is also the author of several books and a contributor to magazines in Europe, Japan, and the United States.*

*The birds in the text are details from an original lithograph by Miró. Courtesy of the Pierre Matisse Gallery.*

# Misuses of the Past

CONTINUED FROM PAGE 12

him to behave himself. He behaved badly enough in the pious Middle Ages. As a product of our own cultural tradition, this cliché might warn us that the immutable human nature we hear about is likely to be the nature of Western man, or rather of some Western men. Many thinkers have assumed in man an inborn, ineradicable greed, a will to power, or an anarchic egotism that the great majority of men in other societies failed to exhibit. The least mutable types in history have been the long-suffering peasant masses, but they hardly look selfish and aggressive in their typically passive, fatalistic endurance; their "depravity" seems more a result of ignorance and inertia than of the old Adam in them. The nature of Americans has been rather different, for better and for worse. And the significant change that seems to be coming over our nature, in the growing conformism of "other-directed" types, also has little to do with the old Adam but much more with the growth of huge organizations and mass media.

Similarly with the worries over the "common man" or the "mass man." He represents problems that we cannot afford to minimize. He also represents a common failing of thinkers, who become victims of their abstractions and forget the infinite variety in type and talent among ordinary people. By definition mediocre, the common man is then made out to be mediocre in *every* respect, and so becomes a statistical monster like the "average man" with 2.5 children. At least he may be decent enough to call for some historical perspective. The so-called "new conservatives," for example, are finding their gods in the great conservatives of the past such as Burke—men who typically had little faith in ordinary human nature, and who may now seem wiser than they were because of the steady succession of failures. We forget that their class had its way throughout most of history. They held the power; they ran the great states and churches; they laid down the law; they set the social standards and goals. The privileged aristocracies and priesthoods that are usually given credit for the great cultural achievements must also bear most of the responsibility for the tragic failures. In their pride they invariably abused their privileges and repeatedly succumbed to the selfishness, greed, and stupidity they feared in the masses.

As we worry over the problems of a mass society and rightly deplore the quality of mass education and mass culture, we might keep in mind the fact that never before in all history have great nations made an effort like that of our own day in the West to educate their entire population and to enable all men to share freely in both their political and cultural life. It is hardly surprising if ordinary men abuse the first real chance they have had in history. Much more surprising, in a historical perspective, is the general acceptance of an idea that many oppose in practice but few would

openly reject: the idea that every man ought to have a fair chance to fulfill himself. The peasant masses in the non-Western world, who still make up the majority of the world's population, are only beginning to get anything like such a chance.

Meanwhile, all our problems may seem worse because traditionalists are always disposed to simplify and falsify the past in the light of their characteristic ideal of stability and certainty. This is an ideal that man has never achieved and can never hope to achieve, short of the death he fears. Traditionalists overlook the basic conditions of man's creative achievements, which include the elementary principle of the inescapable costs of civilization, and more especially of freedom. These costs are implicit in the nature of the only animal that has the power of free, conscious choice, which means the perpetual possibility of foolish or even fatal choices. The costs rose with the rise of civilization, in which an increasing mastery of natural environment brought an increasing dependence on social environment, and in which new material and spiritual goods became new needs, new sources of deprivation and discontent. The costs became still higher as thought became freer, for it raised more questions than it answered, and finally settled nothing. Every major advance in freedom—social, political, intellectual—has meant new problems, including new threats to freedom.

In this view it also becomes important to discredit the popular idea of an automatic, inevitable kind of progress. Such progress as man has made has been only the sporadic realization of new possibilities. His bursts of creativity have always been destructive of cherished values and often fatal to the society that produced them. Nor is further progress guaranteed by any known law of nature, history, or God. It must forever remain uncertain, if man is in any sense free to make history. The painful signs of uncertainty—tension, instability, insecurity, disharmony, conflict—are the essential conditions of possibility, aspiration, idealism. We cannot fully appreciate our extraordinary adventure in freedom unless we realize that it has always been a precarious adventure, demanding the expense of resolute, arduous effort. The full worth of liberty is known only to those who know its full costs. To me, what "history shows" is that its price is indeed eternal vigilance, and that it is worth the effort.

---

*Reversing Lord Acton, Herbert J. Muller writes history but does not teach it. He is Professor of English and Government at Indiana University. His most widely read book is* The Uses of the Past, *but he has also written* Science and Criticism, The Spirit of Tragedy, *and, most recently,* The Loom of History.

# Her Revenge

*By* MARCUS CHEKE

*A tale of passionate rivalry at an Old-world Court when Wagnerian sopranos were in fullest flower*

At the Royal Opera at Friedrichskrone, in the year 1903, were two rival sopranos. Both were equally beautiful, after the somewhat elaborate taste of the day, and the voices of both were equally admired. The one was famed throughout the kingdom as "the Thusnelda"; the other was known as the beautiful Sieglinde. Picture post cards of them, costumed in the part of Manon or Marguerite, were in every shop window. They were paragraphed and photographed in all the daily newspapers. The bouquets of roses, the huge wreaths of gardenias, the pyramids of carnations and lilac wired in the shape of harps or hearts, the slender gilt baskets burdened with exotic blooms handed over the footlights to the Thusnelda at the close of a performance were as innumerable as those which were presented to the Sieglinde; the applause was as deafening and as prolonged. The garrison of the Crown Prince's Hussars, as well as the court itself, was divided into two opposing and equal camps consisting of those who pro-

claimed their devotion to one or the other of the singers. The Thusnelda and the Sieglinde had been the cause of the same incredible number of duels, and together they set the fashions.

Between these two women raged a bitter and intense hatred. Beginning on account of their rivalry on the stage, their mutual jealousy had been further inflamed by their success. In their jewels, in their equipages, which were amongst the most splendid in Friedrichskrone, and in the splendor of their entourage, each attempted to eclipse the other, but in vain. And the single thought that their triumph was not unique poisoned the pleasures of both. Their feelings, therefore, can better be imagined than described when, toward the end of June, the rumor spread that the Grand Duke Alexis of Fürstenhof-Strelitz was shortly to visit the capital for three crowded days of military reviews and maneuvers, and that his visit was to be celebrated by a gala performance at the opera. The piece to be performed was to be *Lohengrin*. The same agonized thought flashed through the minds of both the beautiful Thusnelda and the divine Sieglinde when this news reached them. Who would be chosen to play the main part of Elsa of Brabant on the important night? Both singers knew that there would be no opportunity for them to meet the Grand Duke, as his time would be mapped out to the minute. Each was convinced, on the other hand, that he had only to see her in the part of Elsa to be immediately numbered amongst her conquests.

Nothing had ever been known to equal the intrigues which convulsed the court and the garrisons during the next few days. The claims of the Thusnelda were urged by all her supporters who had access to the throne. The Sieglinde left no stone unturned. Not only did one of her party, a man in a position of the highest distinction, secure the support of the Queen by a suggestion that the King was rather warmly for the Thusnelda, but friends even brought influence to bear upon the Municipal Council, and at a meeting in the Rathaus, tempers became so heated that the representatives of the press were ordered to retire from the building. The Thusnelda succeeded in organizing a deputation to the King from the Charity Commission in her favor. Bets laid upon the result of all this excitement were staggering.

At the end of four days of unbearable tension it was announced that the part of Elsa of Brabant, in the gala performance of *Lohengrin* before the Grand Duke Alexis of

Fürstenhof-Strelitz in two weeks' time, was to be taken by the beautiful Thusnelda. It was said that on hearing of her rival's success the Sieglinde's screams could be heard by passers-by in a street half a mile removed from her villa. But whether or no this story is true, it is certain that she did not for long abandon herself to hysteria, but began at once to plan revenge. There was still a fortnight before the arrival of the Grand Duke.

The Sieglinde published a report of her retirement from Friedrichskrone on account of an indisposition. Her enemies laughed. In reality she did not leave the capital. But she secretly sold her villa, her horses, her pink-upholstered phaeton, her famous golden sleigh, her house at Lendorf, and all her wonderful jewels, and she realized all the money she possessed. She was enormously wealthy. She then sent for eight of the greatest diamond merchants in the world, who came to the small hotel where she was living, always heavily veiled. At the end of five days she had collected a set of precious stones that was probably unequaled even amongst the regalia of prewar Europe.

Now, with the help of a conjurer whom she had known in her childhood, the Sieglinde made these precious stones into a marvelous parure in the crevices of which, between the gems, she placed concealed fireworks. The tiara was of diamonds and pearls. The *rivière* consisted entirely of enormous emeralds; the corsage was encrusted with diamonds, sapphires, and pearls. There were also bracelets of black pearls and brooches of blue diamonds large as the squares on crocodile purses. When it was finished, and when the last of the fireworks had been inserted, the Sieglinde dispatched the jewels to her rival at five o'clock on the evening of the gala performance, which began at eight.

On that memorable night the Opera House at Friedrichskrone had seldom witnessed a more brilliant scene. In the royal box, in addition to the Grand Duke and his hosts, were the Queen of Secklenburg, Prince Joachim Esterhazy, the aged Duchesse de Bourbon, the Archduchess Hélène von Leppel von Serenwälder and Elenore, Freiin zu Weringerode. In a box on the left were the Baron von Meissen and Lord Rosebery. In another sat four of the pretty Lottingen princesses. The stalls were reserved for kings. Frozen into stillness by the first notes of the overture, the wide auditorium assumed suddenly the appearance of some piece of botanical or subaqueous life.

The events which followed are, of course, well known.

ILLUSTRATIONS BY BLAKE HAMPTON

The beautiful Thusnelda, as her angry rival the divine Sieglinde had guessed, was unable to resist the temptation of appearing upon the stage under the weight of £490,000 worth of jewels. And exactly at a quarter of an hour after the first gasp of mingled amazement and bewilderment that her first appearance inspired, the warmth of her body having set the clockwork in motion, and at the very moment when, full throated, she held the center of the stage, and when every eye was fixed upon her, the fireworks went off. Squibs jumped from her brooches; Roman candles flared from her hips; Catherine wheels spun round her breasts; and finally she exploded into a set piece representing the meeting of Bismarck and the king of Prussia after Sedan.

Her discomfiture was complete. Disheveled and half stunned, the Thusnelda rushed from the boards, leaving in her wake, here and there, a dying squib. And the Sieglinde, who was waiting calmly in the wings, was quick to step into her place. Her performance on this occasion was generally considered to have been the performance of her lifetime. The applause which greeted her was more frantic, her bouquets were more numerous than ever.

And yet the Grand Duke Alexis of Fürstenhof-Strelitz, when everybody had left the theater, is said to have gone into the room behind the scenes where the Thusnelda was sobbing alone, her hair singed and her face smeared with burnt gunpowder. It was whispered that he congratulated her solemnly upon the only interpretation of the role of Elsa of Brabant that had ever interested him and that he told her it had been the first occasion on which the opera had not bored him beyond description.

*The foregoing story made its appearance almost thirty years ago in an English review called* Life and Letters. *Its author was then an undergraduate at Trinity College, Oxford. After graduation he entered the British diplomatic service but found time to continue a literary career. While serving at the Lisbon Embassy he wrote* The Life of Marquis de Pombal *and* The Life of Queen Carlota Joaquina. *His latest book, a life of* The Cardinal de Bernis, *has just been published in England. Meanwhile the author has become Sir Marcus Cheke, K.C.V.O., Extra Gentleman Usher to the Queen, and Her Majesty's Minister to the Holy See.*

# CLOUDS ON THE HORIZON

*Edited by* OLIVER JENSEN

THE NEW IDEAL: *A picture post card recently purchased in Sparta by Professor Gilbert Highet.*

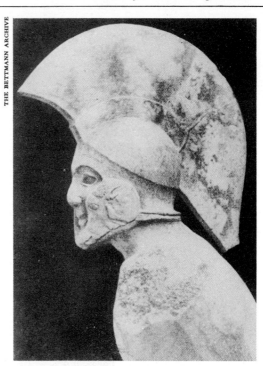

THE OLD IDEAL: *Ancient statue of Leonidas, king of Sparta, who fell at Thermopylae, 480* B.C.

## ALTERATIONS AT SPARTA

"So the Barbarians with Xerxes made the assault [*wrote Herodotus*]; *and the Greeks that were with Leonidas . . . knowing that they should surely die . . . put forth their utmost courage against the barbarians, raging furiously and recking naught. And it hap-pened by that time that most of their spears were already broken; and therefore they slew the Persians with their swords. And in that conflict fell Leonidas, having quitted himself as a brave man, and other notable Spartans with him. . . .*"

## THE AIRLINE AND THE GEISHA

Drumming up trade to the Orient, Northwest Orient Airlines has been offering as a come-on the picture which appears at right. Apparently the traditional Japanese geisha girl is unchanged after all, despite anything one hears to the contrary, and she is still wearing the same getup and playing the same samisen as of yore (see left), but the advertisement does give rise to several tantalizing questions. Who arranges the introductions specified in the caption? The airline? And what about that ridiculous price of $1.81 a day? In *Glimpses of Unfamiliar Japan* (1894), Lafcadio Hearn quotes, from an old geisha song, a passionate suitor's cry:

*Once more the rest beside her, or keep five thousand koku?*
*What care I for koku? Let me be with her!*

The "koku" is a unit of measure in which Japanese once reckoned income, and one koku equals 47.6 gallons or 5.11 bushels. Even allowing for special discounts to passengers, and ignoring ninety years of inflation, $1.81 is quite a drop from 5,000 koku of almost anything. Is there no geisha union? Do the girls make it up in tips? Will the travelers' wives like this? Northwest has some questions to answer, not all of which we have brought up.

Meet charming new friends in a story-book world. Cost of your holiday can be spread out over 20 months (*set aside just $1.81 a day*).

Hair color so natural only her hairdresser knows for sure!

**He says she's the peachiest mom a feller ever had!** She says it's easy to be peachy when you're happy with yourself! And since she's happiest with her looks when her hair is right, she keeps it *beautifully* right with Miss Clairol...the color fresh and natural-looking...the hair itself, silky, sparkling. *Takes only minutes*—and is *so easy* you'll wonder why any woman ever should let gray or fading hair age her looks or dull her outlook.

And now you know why hairdressers all over the world invariably recommend Miss Clairol...and **use it every time to add soft, ladylike, lasting** color to fading hair...to cover gray. With results so sure, why should you wait to look younger... prettier...to feel more attractive! Try Miss Clairol yourself. Today! In wonderful new Creme Formula or Regular.

MISS CLAIROL

Without the text below her picture, you might have some difficulty identifying the lady above. Is she the young man's grade-school teacher? Sister? Dental hygienist? Visiting aunt from Milwaukee? No, she is none of these familiar types, but instead, the most archetypical type of all: that revered image from American popular iconography, pictured in countless ads and illustrations, universally recognized by young and old. She is, in short, MOM—"the peachiest mom," so the caption states, "a feller ever had."

Whatever has happened to Mom? She never used to be like this. She was a dumpy, kindly, apple-cheeked character normally to be found in the kitchen, over which she presided with smiling, softhearted tyranny. She was the one who brushed barefoot boys off the back porch or out of the cookie jar. She was the one who had become an institution so sacred it couldn't be criticized.

But then times changed, and she *was* criticized. Perhaps the most famous disparager of Mom is Philip Wylie, who stridently announced—in *Generation of Vipers* (1942)—that Mom was a fake. Actually, said Wylie, "she is a middle-aged puffin with an eye like a hawk that has just seen a rabbit twitch far below. She is about twenty-five pounds overweight, with no sprint, but sharp heels and a hard backhand. . . . In a thousand of her there is not sex appeal enough to budge a hermit ten paces off a rock ledge."

Apparently Mom took the hint. Surrounded by examples like this, from the back cover of a current fashion magazine, she is ardently trying to be like them—to be thin as a rail, stylish, competent at everything, chummy, ready for a romp with her offspring, and above all sexy. The complications this creates for young Oedipus there, on the right, are best left to the imagination. Perhaps, in an age in which the national number one best seller concerns the romance of a middle-aged man with a twelve-year-old girl, they are no more than we should expect.

WIDE WORLD PHOTOS

## *INNOCENT BYSTANDERS*

Things are very bad for the trolley car all over the world. It has vanished almost overnight from the streets and interurban routes of America, and a whole generation has never seen a streetcar. Barely a dozen U.S. cities have any at all, and of these only Pittsburgh, Washington, and Philadelphia have more than one or two lines. The last old doubledeckers rumbled into the barn in London a few years ago and in many lands the once ubiquitous trolley is becoming something of a curiosity.

But trolleys do have a sort of Valhalla; they get sold down the river to faraway places like India, Rumania, Paraguay, and Pakistan. Cars that once rolled along under the Elevated on 3rd Avenue, New York, now accommodate the swarming millions of Calcutta. But it is clear that the masses do not appreciate the trolley car. In fact, they have an inexplicable dislike for it, and since trolley cars (like old automobiles, cats, postage stamps, and Currier and Ives prints) have their admirers, this makes some people very sad. Observe the picture at left: An angry crowd of sympathizers with Juan Perón, the deposed dictator of Argentina, wished to show their displeasure with the government. *Et quoi?* They burned a number of streetcars. Does the populace set fire to the royal state coach? Do they put flame to the commissar's Zis? No. Even Hitler's old Mercedes survives.

Everywhere this regrettable spirit prevails: Recently in Calcutta followers of rival religions set upon each other. Did they burn each other's houses? No, they burned street-

## BRUSHWORK

To the generations of painters who have prided themselves on the skill and delicacy of their brushwork, the New York school of abstract expressionism has added a new name: Adolph Gottlieb. He is seen at work above on a picture he calls *Ascent*. This is its final form; he is only adding the finishing touches. In Selden Rodman's recent book *Conversations with Artists*, Mr. Gottlieb is quoted as follows: "We are going to have perhaps a thousand years of nonrepresentational painting. . . . Abstraction is not a limitation but a liberation. . . . The social realist wants to charm you or win you over. But the abstract expressionist says to the public (more honestly): 'You're stupid. We despise you. We don't *want* you to like us—or our art. . . .' What is the function of the art school today? To confuse the student. To make a living for the teacher." Mr. Gottlieb teaches art at the Pratt Institute.

cars. And during the riots in Warsaw several years ago how did anti-Soviet crowds express their displeasure with Communism? They burned the streetcars. Is Italy disturbed by religious or political problems? It burns streetcars. Do college boys wish to work off their high spirits? They attack the streetcars. Does the mob hate the regime? The cry is no longer "*Aux lanternes!*"; it is "*Brûlez les tramways.*"

All this is very distressing to those who admire the streetcar, and one can only wonder if some psychiatrist or sociologist or cultural anthropologist or other suitable savant will explain this deplorable quirk in human nature. If the cars get burnt on Monday, what are the survivors going to ride in on Tuesday?

Meanwhile the attention of the authorities is called to what may become a problem fraught with peril. Now that the soapbox is made of cardboard and incapable of supporting an orator; now that the paving block, prime building material of the barricade, has vanished—how, how indeed, if we take away the last trolley, is political action to find its safety valve?

---

### THOUGHT AMONG THE SOCIOLOGISTS

*Q.* What is Professor Talcott Parsons thinking?

*A.* "The Parsonian schema is much more than simply a structural-functional method of analysis. It is an 'action' frame of reference built on a structural-functional base . . . the latest knowledge of motivational processes is combined with modern sociological and anthropological thinking, the whole articulated and given significance on the theoretical and empirical levels in terms of the structural-functional relation. The structure of a social system is formally categorized, and the categories provide the 'morphological' setting within which a 'physiology' of the social system may be developed. The 'dynamic motivational processes' of goal-oriented, role-playing actors interacting in culturally patterned situations—which constitute the independent variables of the system—are located in the structural setting, and the test of their significance is their functional relevance for the maintenance or change of the system." (*from a chapter by Walter Buckley, discussing Professor Talcott Parsons of Harvard, in* Modern Sociological Theory)

*Q.* What is Professor Talcott Parsons thinking?

135

ELEVATION·OF·RIBART'S·ELEPHANT·

# THE
# ELEPHANT
# OF PARIS

To the French, who knew the grandeur of Versailles and the extravagant tastes of the Bourbons, the plans of M. Charles François Ribart in 1758 to build a reception hall in tribute to Louis XV in the shape of an elephant came as merely one more fanciful scheme in an age of fancy. The proposal was entitled *Architecture Singulière: l'Eléphant Triomphal, Grand Kiosque, à la Gloire du Roi* and represented the culmination of the elephant motif in the art and decoration of sixteenth- and seventeenth-century Europe. M. Ribart's elephant will appear in "Architectural Follies in America" by Clay Lancaster, to be published next fall. In describing the spread of elephant architecture, which passed from southeast Asia to Europe and finally to America, Mr. Lancaster writes of Ribart's inspired plan:

"M. Ribart proposed his royal tribute to be set at the terminus of some view, as from the Tuileries up the Champs Elysées to the Etoile. The elephant would bear a tower bristling with a panoply of arms and banners, capped by a statue of his majesty, and elevated on an arcuated platform giving access through vaulted galleries to the wonderful apartments inside the pachyderm itself. A straight flight of steps—the *Grand Escalier*—led up to the first landing, whence one ascended the spiral staircase within a rustic shaft con-

necting with the animal's belly. The kitchen and offices were situated in the lower forequarters of the colossus, their windows concealed by a wide necklace ending in a pendant bell hanging in front of the shoulders. Another flight up the staircase led to the bath—in the hind parts. The principal interior in front was described as an amphitheater to be used for balls, performances, and as a general assembly room. An alcove raised several steps in the head of the elephant provided a place for the throne of the king, with light streaming in through fenestration in the headpiece.

"The last great room to the rear was a banqueting hall, the dome of which, following the contours of the elephant's back, was to be treated in the manner of a forest glen, with trees and vines masking its limits, and having a brook encircling the room, incorporating a series of cascades, the water emptying into the bath underneath. A winding path (in reality a narrow stairway) ascended from the dining room to a small card room over the stair well. The elephant was supposed to be quenching his thirst, but instead the uplifted end of his snout regurgitated water into a tank, witnessed by a bevy of mermaids. As it happened, M. Ribart's masterpiece never materialized to honor Louis XV or any other ruler."